DARK VALLEYS

WHEN YOU LOVE JESUS BUT HATE LIFE

TODD M. SMITH

LUCIDBOOKS

ISBN-10: 1-63296-167-9
ISBN-13: 978-1-63296-167-9
eISBN-10: 1-63296-168-7
eISBN-13: 978-1-63296-168-6

This book is dedicated to my father,
Richard M. Smith.
Keeping his eye on the Shepherd, he guided
me through many of life's valleys.

Table of Contents

Acknowledgments

A short, frankly inadequate, page to sufficiently say thank you:

Thank you to my Shepherd, Jesus Christ, without whom nothing is possible, let alone the writing of a book.

Thank you to Lucid Publishing, who directed and believed in this first-time writer. Your team is the bomb! To Matt Erickson and David Gregory for your editorial giftedness. To Debbie Reed for your professional insight and to Debbie Abramson for your sacrifice of time to make this book read so much better.

Thank you to Crossroads, the most patient, life-giving church and staff who seek weekly to kick a dent in eternity because they just get it. To a faithful, wise, and encouraging elder board—men who are everything the Scriptures ask of shepherds—I'm so grateful for your faithfulness.

Most importantly, I want to thank my kids and my amazing wife, Stacey. I have chased you since you were twelve, and you still take my breath away every time you walk into the room.

Introduction

There was shame on his face and in his voice.

"Pastor Todd, I have never been able to tell someone inside the church that I struggle with depression." I must have looked shocked because he quickly tried to justify why he could not share this with another believer. The whole time, I kept thinking of the words of Jesus in Matthew 11:28–30:

> *Come to me, all who labor and are heavy laden, and I will give you rest. Take my yoke upon you, and learn from me, for I am gentle and lowly in heart, and you will find rest for your souls. For my yoke is easy, and my burden is light.*

The real tragedy here is not my friend's depression but the fact that this godly man was ashamed of his depression. You see, this guy is a real Christian, not a Christmas and Easter Christian, which I call a "Creaster." No, this guy loves Jesus and believes in the sufficiency and inerrancy of the Scriptures. He even has a John Calvin T-shirt (okay, that's an exaggeration). Yet he was ashamed he was depressed.

As he continued to share with me, I could also hear fear in his voice; he was afraid of people at his church finding out he was depressed. As if being depressed is not enough, let's make people anxious about being depressed. Let's shame them into silence because that is what Jesus would do, right? I wanted to scream out that day like the apostle Paul, "May it never be!" (Rom. 3:4 NASB).

Okay, but why did I write a book on Christian depression?

Well, news flash! I am the last person who should have written this book. I am a pastor, not a writer. I have had seasons of depression, but I am not a depressed person. I don't see myself as a counselor. In fact, I often say to my congregation that if you come to me for counseling, all I am going to say is "Stop it!" I never rank that high on personality tests in the areas of compassion and understanding.

So why did I write it? Why did I write my first book, possibly my only book, on Christian depression?

Because the silence on this topic is deafening.

The debates continue to rage: Is depression all physical or all spiritual? These mind-numbing debates are hurting people who are already hurting and offering no hope and no help in their distress. Our brothers and sisters in Christ are carrying burdens they should not have to carry alone.

Let me share how this became so clear to me that I decided I had to write this book. In the spring of 2016, I stumbled across a new book on Charles Spurgeon. I love this preaching giant. He would be on the Mount Rushmore of preaching if there were one. I had always known he was melancholy at times, but I had no idea that he suffered from depression. The book is called *Spurgeon's Sorrows* and was written by Pastor Zack Eswine. I was stunned to read Spurgeon's own words about his dark battle with depression. Here is a man whose writings I studied in seminary. He was a man who knew God in a very real and deep way, yet he had a real thorn in the flesh called depression.

So that spring, I decided to write a blog post about depression, a simple 617-word blog post. My blog is mainly read by family, my dog, my wife, and a few others. The plan was to bless a handful of regular readers on the topic of Christian depression. Well, that was only until I hit the publish button for this blog post I called "Christian Depression: Be Helpful, Not Hurtful."

Within hours, it traveled to more than 40 countries, and the blog platform I use kept alerting me to heavy traffic on my blog. For the next 30 days, I received e-mails, texts, private messages, and cards saying thank you for writing on this topic. Even strangers came up to me in Starbucks and thanked me. After thanking me, they would share an excruciating story of how they or someone they love is fighting a real and daily battle with depression. They explained how they love Jesus and want victory, but they still experience more losses than wins in this battle. And the kicker was that most of them said they rarely share their struggles with any of their Christian friends. No wonder they are struggling!

During those spring days, I heard story after story of people who really love Jesus but just hate life right now. Most of the help they got was in the form of advice from two vastly different perspectives:

- More prayer or more pills
- More Scripture or more substances

- More church or more counseling
- More truth or more therapy
- More creeds or more chemistry

Yet they were dying because no one was helping them. Lots of debates, studies, and opinions, but no real encouragement or compassion. Most had to pay people to help them. Nothing is wrong with paying a good Christian counselor, but what about the church? What about the family of God? Sure, they can read the articles on so-called quick fixes, but no one was really offering to walk with them. No one helped shepherd them through the valley and into a real place of hope.

God's timing is always perfect. When I wrote that blog, I had recently completed a study of Psalm 23. I worked my way through this majestic psalm, seeing our Shepherd in a new and fresh way, a way I had never seen him before. Then the "aha moment" hit me: There is no way out of the valley, but there is a way *through* the valley of depression. The Good Shepherd will walk us through the valley. *The way out is the way through.*

Psalm 23 offers those who battle with depression real hope. The Shepherd is not going to let you die in the valley. We must look and listen for the voice of the Shepherd. He is the way through the dark days of depression. He leads, he guides, and he restores. He can find you a green pasture and some still waters. Scripture reminds us that we have a very good Shepherd. He is a Shepherd who will take every single step with his sheep through the valley. Fixing your mind on Christ is a step toward fixing your mind.

> **Fixing your mind on Christ is a step toward fixing your mind.**

So what do you need during your time in the valley? I have spent a lot of time with sheep. As a shepherd, I pastor a great flock with real needs. I have learned that we all have scars under our skin that tell a story. All of humanity has deep tissue bruising. My experience in working with sheep is that we all need a few things while in the valley of depression. Here are the basic common needs I believe this book offers.

We need hope. Everyone needs hope, but especially those in depression. This book is going to give you hope. There is a way through this valley. There is a new kind of normal coming. God's grace is sufficient, and his mercies are new every morning. Your hope comes from the fact that you plus the Good Shepherd are a profound majority.

We need real help. This is not a self-help book offering another seven steps to happiness that won't really work. You need a Shepherd who can lead, guide, and restore you. The journey will take time, and there is no quick fix, but there is help on the way.

We need humility. This book is going to ask you to humble yourself and give yourself permission to accept your struggles. Acceptance means it is time to stop playing games. Games belong in boxes, not in your life. This means you must be willing to accept and acknowledge that your struggle is real and that you cannot defeat it alone.

We need healing. Jesus is our Redeemer, and he is really good at what he does. He redeems people and their lives, and he brings healing. You will get through the valley; you will not die in the valley. You are going to be okay.

Lastly, we need holiness. That is God's plan for all of us—to share in his holiness as Hebrews 12:10 states:

> For they disciplined us for a short time as it seemed best to them, but he disciplines us for our good, that we may share his holiness.

But we aren't talking about a holiness that is generated by self-effort. There's a good chance you've tried that and failed. We're talking about a holiness that he works into us as we learn to rest in his love, experience his full grace, and walk in true dependence on the One who, we will come to learn, always wants the very best for us.

I don't know the way God will bring you out of your depression, but we can walk through it together with him. Together we will feed ourselves with Psalm 23. This will be our guide through the valley.

> The LORD is my Shepherd; I shall not want.
> He makes me lie down in green pastures.
> He leads me beside still waters.
> He restores my soul.
> He leads me in paths of righteousness
>   for his name's sake.
> Even though I walk through the valley of the
>   shadow of death,
>   I will fear no evil,
> for you are with me;
>   your rod and your staff,
>   they comfort me.
> You prepare a table before me
>   in the presence of my enemies;

you anoint my head with oil;
my cup overflows.
Surely goodness and mercy shall follow me
all the days of my life,
and I shall dwell in the house of the LORD
forever.

The great news is that together we are going to meet the One who can get you through the valley. There is real hope in the midst of the darkness. You see, our Shepherd is called the Good Shepherd for a reason. He will see you through your valley.

Yes, he will.

I am looking forward to this journey together.

Pastor Todd

THE VALLEY OF DEPRESSION

Fits of depression come over the most of us. Usually cheerful as we may be, we must at intervals be cast down. The strong are not always vigorous, the wise not always ready, the brave not always courageous, and the joyous not always happy.

—Charles Spurgeon

CHAPTER ONE

Life in the Valley

He drew me up from the pit of destruction,
out of the miry bog,
and set my feet upon a rock,
making my steps secure.

—Psalm 40:2

You are not alone.

Did you know that Abraham Lincoln, Alan Alda, Terry Bradshaw, Barbara Bush, Winston Churchill, Ernest Hemingway, John D. Rockefeller, Princess Diana, Martin Luther, Emily Dickinson, Robin Williams, and Mark Twain all suffered from bouts of depression? What a group!

You may be surprised to learn that Abraham Lincoln wrote the following words:

> I am now the most miserable man living. If what I feel were equally distributed to the whole human family, there would not be one cheerful face on the earth. Whether I shall ever be better I can not tell; I awfully forebode I shall not. To remain as I am is impossible; I must die or be better, it appears to me.

President Lincoln's words hit close to home for many— including me, including you.

We already mentioned Charles Spurgeon. He is regarded by many as the greatest preacher of all time— the "prince of preachers." For 40 years of the 19th century, before the age of microphones, Spurgeon preached to 5,000 people at a time at the Metropolitan Tabernacle in London. He was a prolific author, publishing more than 150 books. Over 300 million copies of Spurgeon's written works have been printed worldwide. He was possibly the person most greatly used by God in the 19th century.

He also battled chronic depression, severe depression that troubled him his entire life.

It started when he was 24 years old. He later recalled, "My spirits were sunken so low that I could weep by the hour like a child, and yet I knew not what I wept for." He fought a lifelong battle against what he called his "causeless depression," describing it as a "shapeless, undefinable, yet all-beclouding hopelessness" that "is not to be reasoned with." Over the course of 40 years of ministry, on average Spurgeon failed to show up in his own pulpit one of every three Sundays due to depression and other ailments.[1]

He was a man greatly used by God but one who spent a good deal of his life walking through what David described as "the valley of the shadow of death" (Ps. 23:4).

Spurgeon walked through his valleys. I have good news for you. You *can* get through your valley, too.

Before we go any further, I want you to know that before you even picked this book up, I have been praying for you. I prayed this book would land in the hands of people who need it at just the right time. I don't think this moment is an accident, but rather a divine appointment. And I am praying, whether it is a page or a paragraph, that God will use it to help you in those dark valley days of life.

Depression is real, even for Christians

Depression is real. It is real for all people, those who don't follow Jesus and those who do. It is part of the human condition.

The US Centers for Disease Control and Prevention reports that at any given moment, 8% of the population in the United States suffers from depression.[2] The Association of Certified Biblical Counselors also states that "over eighty million people, meaning one in four Americans, will meet the criteria for major depression in their lifetime."[3]

Your chance of winning the lottery is about one in 14 million. Your chance of experiencing genuine depression is about one in four. Listen, the likelihood of depression washing ashore in your life is high and almost guaranteed to hit someone you deeply care about. You are not alone.

Christian depression

Anyone who thinks there are no Christians among those one in four people has their head in the sand. Christians get depressed, too. Look at Charles Spurgeon. Or, even better, look at the slew of people in the Bible who went through great seasons of depression. If you haven't noticed them, you might not have been paying close enough attention. Moses, David, Elijah, Naomi, Job, Hannah, Jeremiah, Jonah, Mary, Martha, Paul, Timothy, and many others all experienced periods of sorrow and sadness.

And why should that surprise us?

If there is one thing the Bible is, it is real about life. There is no photo-shopped Christianity in the Scriptures. And as the Spirit of God moved the biblical writers to pen their accounts, he made this clear: the Christian life has many dark valleys. Even our Savior said, "In the world you will have tribulation" (John 16:33). Jesus never guesses; he only knows. He knew well that life in this world can kick your teeth in.

A depressed Christian is not a fictional figure created by Pixar. You really can love Jesus and find yourself hating life. Maybe that's why the Scriptures have so much to say about depression. Proverbs, part of the wisdom literature of the Bible, gives expression to the experience of depression. Just listen to the writer in Proverbs 17:22: *"A joyful heart is good medicine, but a crushed spirit dries up the bones."* And in Proverbs 18:14 (KJV), he says, *"The spirit of a man will sustain his infirmity; but a wounded spirit who can bear?"*

Words like *"crushed," "dried up,"* and *"wounded spirit"* express the feelings of those struggling with depression. Charles Spurgeon referred to his depression as his "heaviness." This is a great description of depression—a heaviness. As we saw in Proverbs, the weight of depression can crush the human soul.

Throughout Scripture, the Bible is very clear and accurate in the physical effects of those who experience depression:

- Disturbed sleep – Job 7:4, 13–15
- Physical tiredness – Psalm 6:6; 69:3
- Weight fluctuations – Job 17:7; 19:20
- Digestive problems – Lamentations 3:15
- Loss of appetite – Psalm 42:3; 102:4
- Bodily pain – Psalm 31:10; 32:3–4; 38:3
- Choking feelings and breathlessness – Psalm 69:1–2

Usually a person's greatest wounds are invisible to the naked eye. The bruising and brokenness is deep within. If your own bruising manifests as depression, you are not alone in your struggle. The statistics tell us that. But more importantly, you are not alone in the grand scheme of things. God tells us that. He loves you from eternity past (Jer. 31:3). He has not and will never, ever abandon you (Heb. 13:6). He is our Good Shepherd who says he "is near to the brokenhearted" (Ps. 34:18), whether you feel it in this season of your life or not. He does not lie to us.

What is depression?

People may ask, is depression just a bad case of being sad? No, sadness and depression are not the same. You can be sad but not depressed. Sadness is a temporary emotion or feeling that comes and goes. Sad feelings are like buses; a new one comes every ten minutes. Sadness can be like a meteor that goes shooting across the sky and is gone. But depression settles in and soaks into the human soul.

Depression is a deep soul reaction that includes intense feelings of helplessness and hopelessness. These feelings are the symptoms of something going on inside a person. The waves of feelings may last for many weeks or longer. They can become so intense that they actually keep you from functioning like you normally would each day.

Clinically speaking, the American Psychiatric Association's *Diagnostic and Statistical Manual of Mental Disorders, 5th Edition* describes what qualifies a person for a diagnosis of major depressive episode. Five (or more) of the following symptoms must be present during the same two-week period and represent a change from previous functioning; at least one of the symptoms must be either (1) depressed mood or (2) loss of interest or pleasure.

1. Depressed mood most of the day, nearly every day, as indicated by either subjective report (e.g., feels sad, empty, hopeless) or observation made by others (e.g., appears tearful). (*Note*: In children and adolescents, can be irritable mood.)
2. Markedly diminished interest or pleasure in all, or almost all, activities most of the day, nearly every day (as indicated by either subjective account or observation).
3. Significant weight loss when not dieting or weight gain (e.g., a change of more than 5 percent of body weight in a month) or a decrease or increase in appetite nearly

every day. (*Note:* In children, consider failure to make expected weight gain.)

4. Insomnia or hypersomnia nearly every day.
5. Psychomotor agitation or retardation nearly every day (observable by others, not merely subjective feelings of restlessness or being slowed down).
6. Fatigue or loss of energy nearly every day.
7. Feelings of worthlessness or excessive or inappropriate guilt (which may be delusional) nearly every day (not merely self-reproach or guilt about being sick).
8. Diminished ability to think or concentrate, or indecisiveness nearly every day (either by subjective account or as observed by others).
9. Recurrent thoughts of death (not just fear of dying), recurrent suicidal ideation without a specific plan, or a suicide attempt or a specific plan for committing suicide.[4]

You will notice that clinical depression is something that stays with us and is not easily shaken. Some describe it as getting stuck, which is why saying to yourself or another, "Hey, just get over it" does not help.

An example I use to explain what depression can be like is vinyl records. I came of age in the greatest decade ever, the 80s. This means I grew up on records and record players. (Yes, they were still being used in the 80s!) Remember the needle on that record player? You would place it onto the black space of the outer rim of the record (unless you were rich and had one of those automatic ones). Over time, dust would build up in the grooves of the record and on the needle. When this happened, the needle would get stuck in a groove and play the same lyric over and over again.

Depression can feel much like the needle and the groove. Over time, the needle of your life picks up dust and gets stuck in a groove. You just can't move past a particular lyric or point in your life. Your life becomes a rut. A rut is simply a grave with the ends knocked out.

> A rut is simply a grave with the ends knocked out.

Underlying root of depression

The root cause of depression is original sin, the total depravity of man. Depression is not sin, but depression is the result of original sin. Let me explain.

I am not a clinician. I am not a medical doctor. I am not a psychologist. I am not a psychiatrist. I am a shepherd. I am a pastor. I am PT (Pastor Todd), not Dr. Todd. A person should see their physician in the early days of depression to rule out any organic triggers for their depression. While there are many possible triggers to depression, I am primarily interested in the theological roots of depression.

Depression triggers can vary greatly. People don't become depressed for no reason. Usually the trigger is obvious, but sometimes there are deeper layers that may not be so obvious. The Bible answers the macro question as to the origin of our brokenness. Death, disease, and, yes, even depression come from the fact that we are fallen beings who live in a fallen world.

What does that mean? It means that the effects of sin, of humanity's rebellion against God, have radically infected everything about our lives. We came from sinners, we were born into the world as sinners, and if we have children, we have given birth to sinners. Not only have our lives been infected, all of creation has been infected, too (Rom. 8:22). Nothing in this world has escaped being terribly marred by sin. Just reading the morning headlines will confirm that.

In Genesis 2:7, the Bible tells us, "Then the Lord God formed the man of dust from the ground and breathed into his nostrils the breath of life, and the man became a living creature." The dust became the physical body, and the breath of God became man's soul.

But both body and soul were susceptible from the beginning to what we call sin. We know this because God warned the first man that on the day he disobeyed God's command, "you will surely die" (Gen. 2:17). And that day came when man disobeyed. He did not immediately die physically, but now his days were numbered. He died spiritually immediately, being separated from his connection to God, and death began working in his body immediately, culminating in his physical death years later.

On November 15, 1998, I experienced the worst day of my life. The same day, my father experienced the best day of his life. He stepped into Heaven and I stepped into a funeral home. The year leading up to that autumn day in 1998, we watched on MRI after MRI the cancer spreading throughout his body. It was like watching a devilish Pac-Man. This Pac-Man monster traveled into every part of his body. I can still see the MRI of his brain with all those cancerous tumors.

Sin in humanity is a lot like cancer—a monster that has spread into every cell of the human body and soul. It leaves nothing untouched. It does not discriminate; it visits every zip code in the world. It is a beast that makes things die. My dad's death certificate said cancer was the cause, but don't be fooled: what killed him was sin. Again,

I am not saying my dad's personal sins, which we all have, led to his death; I am saying that sin, which has infected all of humanity, leads to all death.

So sin affects not just our spiritual lives but also our physical lives and our emotional lives. It affects our liver, kidneys, lungs, and, yes, even our brains, the most complex organ in our body. In this way, it is theologically correct to say all depression is a result of the fall.

Understanding depression's origin helps us avoid two simplistic extremes.

The first extreme is claiming that all depression is all spiritual in its origin. Therefore, the solution is to just take this verse and see me in the morning. Or just pray more. Or just read the Bible more, and it will go away. Treating depression can be more complex than "just do this." We are made of soul and body, and these are interconnected. God designed us that way. What happens in our soul affects our body, and what happens in our body affects our soul. The fall of humanity into sin has desperately affected both soul and body. Treating depression requires a both-and, not an either-or approach. You may need a good doctor, a godly counselor, medication, and a gracious life-giving church family.

The other extreme reaction is claiming that the problem of depression is all physical—we just need to fix our neurons and synapses. Just get on the right meds, and all will be fine. Antidepressants are available, and they can be of great benefit when necessary and properly used. But there is no pill that produces happiness or holiness. Maybe it would be nice if there were, and certainly Americans seem to buy pharmaceuticals as if they could do that. There are more than 250 million prescriptions written in the United States each year. At more than $10 billion per year, our pharmaceutical sales for depression are greater than the entire economies of 74 nations combined. But depression is more complex than neurons, synapses, and chemicals, and taking a pill to fix what may be wrong with them does not address the sorrow and emptiness in our souls.

Sadly, many non-believers are only treated with chemicals, and they really need conversion. For Christians, there will often need to be a balance between medicines for the brain, rest for the body, counsel for the mind, and spiritual encouragement for the soul. People's lives, including Christians, can be improved with medication. Shaming a Christian for receiving God's grace in the form of medication is wrong on many levels. If you are a man who does not think chemicals inside your body affect you, then ask your wife if she thinks chemicals inside her body affect her.

Don't fall into the all-or-nothing thinking. Once again, in some situations, it is a both-and, not an either-or decision. But for the Christian, taking antidepressants is never a substitute for what Peter wrote in 2 Peter 3:18: "But grow in the grace and knowledge of our Lord and Savior Jesus Christ." Even with medical help, Christians must learn to let Jesus be their Good Shepherd and to follow him closely.

However, the sad truth is that depression has not always been met with compassion in the church.

Improper responses by the church

Christian depression is not an oxymoron. I hope that is apparent by now.

If God is near to the brokenhearted, won't his people, the church, automatically be near to them, too? Unfortunately, no. Not nearly often enough.

When was the last time you heard someone share publicly at church that they were depressed? Probably not recently, if ever. Church is not a place where people typically admit to such struggles. Yet God designed the church as a hospital for souls, not a hotel for the healthy. And there are silent sufferers in the pews of our churches. They are depressed and ashamed to speak about it.

Although this has been changing somewhat the last couple of decades, too often Christians have one of three inappropriate responses to those suffering from depression. The first is denial as they attempt to ignore it. To them, depression is a mirage—the imaginings of a confused mind. Without being too harsh, such beliefs are ignorant and insensitive. Spurgeon addressed a type of such dismissal with these words: "Reader, never ridicule the nervous and hypochondriacal, their pain is real; though much of the malady lies in the imagination, thought-processes, it is not imaginary."[5]

Other Christians simply dismiss it as they attempt to shrink its significance or impact. They have never experienced significant depression, either in themselves or in the life of someone else they are close to. When you put the word *Christian* next to the word *depression,* those who dismiss depression give you the fish eye. They think, *How could someone filled with the Spirit of God, who is there to produce the fruit of joy in their lives, possibly be depressed?* So they simply deny the existence or shrink the significance.

Finally, many in the church not only deny and dismiss the possibility of a Christian struggling with depression but also distance themselves from the situation. This can be for many reasons. They may not know what to say or fear that depression may be contagious. Sadly, the attempt to detach themselves may be because they see depression as self-inflected by the person's sin, thinking, "You get what you deserve." Anyone so depressed, they reason, must be mired in sin and has chosen to camouflage their sin by calling it depression. Sinful behavioral patterns may have nothing to do with a person's depression. But even if they do, what excuse is that for believers to abandon one another? Jesus said he came not for the healthy but for the sick—those spiritually sick from sin. That includes all of us.

Denial, dismissal, or detachment are all ways to avoid the problem as well as the sufferers. This thinking is not just improper, it is dangerous. More than 38,000 Americans die by suicide each year—that's more than 100 people per day. The church, which is you and I, cannot afford to deny, dismiss, or become detached from those suffering with depression. Depression can have serious consequences. If our Savior draws near to the brokenhearted, we dare not abandon them ourselves.

So let's all agree we can do better in the areas of compassion and care. The depressed need them both.

Goal of this book

This book is a modest attempt to come alongside those of you who suffer from depression and to help you walk through the dark valley. This book is not a quick fix or a thin veneer of positive thinking. I am not an expert in the field, but I come across a lot of people suffering with depression. This book is written by a shepherd about following the Good Shepherd in the seasons of sadness and sorrow. I spend most of my time with sheep. And I know this: sheep get messy. This book is written for sheep—sheep who struggle with seasons of depression.

This book is also for the spouses, parents, adult children, friends, and coworkers of such sufferers. You want to understand what is happening with him or her, and you'd love to be an encourager without being trite. I believe this book can help. We all need one another, and what I discuss here can help you be there for others in an uplifting way.

Before we embark together on this journey, let me lay out three basic assumptions that people suffering from depression should affirm as we start.

First, if you suffer with depression, you are not alone. I spend my days, weeks, and months helping people walk through the valley of the shadow of death. This life is not meant to be walked alone. You have people in your life who care deeply, even if imperfectly, about you. Most importantly, you have a Savior, a Good Shepherd, who cares deeply about you.

Second, realize that there is a way through this season. My desire is to connect you to the Good Shepherd so he can lead you through your valley.

Recently, my family spent a few days in Yosemite National Park. (God becomes really big and life becomes really small looking up at a creation like Half Dome.) I considered myself wise for not paying for one of those overpriced tours of the park. We could find our own way around, thank you, and probably discover some gems that no tour would show us. Wrong. By the end of our time at Yosemite, I realized it sure would have been nice to have someone guide us through the valley. There would have been fewer wasted steps. We could have seen so much more and learned so much more along the journey with the help of a guide.

You are in a valley. We all go through valleys. Some of us go through really deep ones. As you travel through, don't make the same mistake I made in Yosemite. Invite along a guide. This book can serve as a helpful guide because I am simply seeking to point you to your true Guide. I want to compel you to get behind the Shepherd. He will faithfully lead you through the valley in such a way that you will not just emerge on the other side but grow in ways you never thought were possible in your time of distress.

Which leads me to the third thing we can affirm. I write to remind you that there are no wasted tears when you follow Jesus. The psalmist writes this in Psalm 56:8:

> *You have kept count of my tossings;*
> *put my tears in your bottle.*
> *Are they not in your book?*

He reminds us that the tears of God's kids are precious to him. The Father even saw his own son with a tear-stained face. Spurgeon said, "A Jesus who never wept could never wipe away my tears."[6] This book is all about the Chief Shepherd, our Lord, and his desire to meet you in the midst of your depression and walk with you. Jesus is our Redeemer. That means he can redeem even the most difficult parts of our lives and bring something good out of them.

This book is oil for the hardened scabs of pain; it is a green pasture for the weary; it is still water for the thirsty. So, young mom, college student alone in the dorm, venture capitalist, single young adult, empty nester with extra bedrooms, and missionary struggling far from home, this book is for you because the Shepherd is with you. This book is for all those whose lives have been touched by depression.

Through the valley with the Good Shepherd

We are all on a journey. Some of that journey is fun and pleasant. Some of it is not. Depression is definitely not. Jesus knows that. He knows what it is like to suffer. He is a man of sorrows. He wants to walk with and lead us through the valley of depression. He is our Good Shepherd, not our German Shepherd, and he is the expert at helping others carry heavy burdens (Matt. 11:28).

This book is for those who desire to follow the Shepherd not just to the mountaintops, but also through the valleys. It is for those seeking to trust the Good Shepherd, for those who need to know he has not abandoned them.

No matter what has gotten you into the valley, the Good Shepherd will lead you through it.

You are not alone.

You are not crazy.

But you must keep walking.

CHAPTER TWO

King David Knew Dark Days Too

I am weary with my moaning; every night I flood my bed with tears; I drench my couch with my weeping.

—Psalm 6:6

As we look at God's perspective on depression in the Bible, we need a personal guide. It needs to be someone who has experienced depression firsthand, has laid hold of God's truth concerning his or her depression, and has actually successfully lived out that truth.

Maybe you know someone like that in your own life, but I'm thinking about someone a little older. Like 3,000 years older. The Bible itself has the perfect candidate to be our guide. He may or may not have experienced more depression than anyone in the Scriptures, but he certainly wrote about it more than anyone else.

Who is our guide going to be? King David.

When you think of David, depression is probably not the first thing that comes to your mind. You're more likely to think of David's defeat of Goliath, his victorious kingship, his psalms of praise, or possibly his sin with Bathsheba. However, David struggled with depression—a lot. Events in his life gave him ample reason to be very down for very long periods of time.

It starts when King Saul, jealous of David's popularity after his defeat of Goliath, begins throwing spears at him in the royal palace. When David is about 25, Saul banishes him from the royal court and then decides to gather his soldiers and hunt David down to kill him.

David stays on the run from Saul for close to a decade—a decade!—hiding in caves and fleeing to such places as Gath, a city of the Philistines, his mortal enemies. Again and again, he barely escapes with his life. Saul kills almost 100 priests of God who had helped David and his band of men. David is betrayed multiple times, but each time God delivers him. Since David stays away from Jerusalem so long, Saul gives David's wife, Michel, in marriage to another man. Saul finally dies in a battle with Israel's enemies, as does David's closest friend of 20 years, Saul's son Jonathan.

After David is made king of the southern kingdom of Judah, the northern kingdom of Israel wages war against him for more than five years. After the entire kingdom is united under his kingship, David succumbs to temptation and sleeps with Bathsheba. He commits murder to cover up his sin. The infant that is born to him dies. Two years later, David's son Amnon rapes his half-sister, Tamar. David's son Absalom, brother of Tamar, murders Amnon. David has to banish him. Absalom ends up fomenting civil war against David. David has to flee his own palace. In the war, Absalom is killed.

This list even *leaves out* some significant things in David's life that would plunge any of us into depression. Over and over, David experienced devastating heartbreak, grief, and despair—events best described as jaw-dropping disappointment. Can you relate?

Fortunately for us, David didn't hide his discouragement, depression, and despair. Those themes run all through the 73 psalms that he penned. Interesting to note is that the Hebrew word for *psalm* means "book of praise." The problem is that once you open the book of Psalms, you realize quickly that well over half of the psalms are psalms of lament—hardly truth in advertising!

Here are but a few samples of David's laments:

> *I am weary with my moaning; every night I flood my bed with tears; I drench my couch with my weeping.*
>
> —Psalm 6:6

How long, O Lord? Will you forget me forever?
How long will you hide your face from me?
How long must I take counsel in my soul,
And have sorrow in my heart all the day?

—Psalm 13:1–2

My God, My God, why have you forsaken me?
Why are you so far from saving me, from the words
of my groaning?
O my God, I cry by day, but you do not answer,
and by night, but I find no rest.

—Psalm 22:1–2

Be gracious to me, O Lord, for I am in distress;
my eye is wasted from grief;
my soul and my body also.
For my life is spent with sorrow,
and my years with sighing.

—Psalm 31:9–10a

I sink in deep mire,
where there is no foothold;
I have come into deep waters,
and a flood sweeps over me.
I am weary with my crying out;
my throat is parched.
My eyes grow dim
with waiting for my God.

—Psalm 69:2–3

Therefore my spirit faints within me;
my heart within me is appalled.

—Psalm 143:4

David was a man who *knew* depression. More than 50 times in the Psalms, David declares his dark night of the soul with words like these:

> *I am troubled.*
> *I am bowed down greatly.*
> *I go mourning all day long.*
> *I groan because of the turmoil of my heart.*

Some of his depression arose from sinful choices that he made and the consequences he suffered. Some of his depression had nothing to do with his own choices. It resulted from some exceedingly difficult circumstances forced upon him.

What did David's depression produce in him? Psalm 6 gives us many clues. First, David's depression produced physical symptoms:

> *Be gracious to me, O Lord, for I am languishing;*
> *heal me, O Lord, for my bones are troubled.*
> > —Psalm 6:2

David's very bones could feel the weight of his depression. In depression, there is a direct connection between body and soul that can be clearly felt. David experienced bone-deep feelings of despair. Being depressed can feel like a physical disorder because it is so exhausting and because the body itself can hurt.

David's depression produced fear and doubt.

> *My soul also is greatly troubled.*
> *But you, O Lord—how long?*
> *Turn, O Lord, deliver my life;*
> *save me for the sake of your steadfast love.*
> > —Psalm 6:3–4

Our word *worry* comes from a German word meaning "to choke." This can be exactly how depression feels. David was greatly troubled; he felt as if he was being choked and losing perspective. Depression can heighten our fears and trigger anxieties.

David's depression produced a sense of hopelessness.

> *For in death there is no remembrance of you;*
> *in Sheol who will give you praise?*
> —Psalm 6:5

Depression eats hope for breakfast. Depression breeds despair. David is fearful for his life—a feeling of great despair. When we are depressed, we can experience such despair that we believe our lives are over and there is no turning back. When hope is lost, it feels as though life itself is lost. David had lost purpose for his life, and there appeared to be no way out or a way through for him.

Depression produces a host of other symptoms. It can sharpen the point of all of our emotions, making everything seem like more than we can bear. Depression can make you feel everything or nothing at all. It distorts reality, producing a mental grid through which everything looks black. It produces a sense of isolation, even if we are surrounded by people. All these symptoms show up in David's laments.

There is very good news about David's depression, however. It never got the last word in David's life. We know this because of God's own assessment of him. Despite David's depression, his many weaknesses, his failings, and his many bad choices, God still called David "a man after my heart" and said that he "served the purpose of God in his own generation" (Acts 13:22, 36). *That* was God's assessment of David.

The fact that David was God's heart-chaser was revealed not in David avoiding depression but rather in how he responded to it. He let it usher him into the presence of God. He let it teach him to cry out to God and trust more deeply in God. When depressed over significant sins, David always repented.

Because David let his depression drive him to God, not away from God, he really did fulfill God's purpose in his own generation. Consequently, David is the ideal guide for us. He knows the depths of this valley, and he knows how God wants us to walk through the valley with him. He knows how to let God use the valley to mold us into the people he is making us to be.

Time to prep for the trip

Here is where you need to take inventory.

David made it through the valley. He walked, not ran, through it. David never gave up. He never quit. He always fell forward. David's life shows a consistent pattern of how he responded to his time in the valley. His actions of running to God can guide you in responding to the darkness as well. Like David, you must sit and stay in the valley when every cell in your body is telling you to self-motivate or self-medicate.

Here are three trip preparation essentials that David used to get through the valley. With each, I have provided a personal application to help you begin to align yourself with what God wants you to be doing in this difficult time of your life.

Prepping for a trip is as important as the trip itself. Take time to prepare.

1. David cried out; you cry out

In my distress, I called upon the Lord;
to my God I cried for help.
From his temple, he heard my voice,
and my cry to him reached his ears.

—Psalm 18:6

In times of desperation, David cries out to God—loudly. The Hebrew word for "crying out" (*za`aq*) means "crying out, very loudly." It's loud enough to be heard in the next county (Isa. 15:4), as when soldiers cry out so loudly that their voices are heard above the heat of battle (1 Chron. 5:20).

Listen to David as he cries out in Psalm 38:1–2:

O LORD, rebuke me not in your anger,
nor discipline me in your wrath!
For your arrows have sunk into me,
and your hand has come down on me.

David says something like this to the Lord: "You are crushing me, and I can barely handle this experience."

Hear David weep in Psalm 142:1–3:

With my voice I cry out to the Lord;
with my voice, I plead for mercy to the Lord.
I pour out my complaint before him;
I tell my trouble before him.
When my spirit faints within me,
you know my way!

David doesn't water down or paint over his struggle and pain. David pulls the complaint card with the Lord of creation. David is sincere in the midst of his pain.

David didn't bottle any stuff. His heart was an open book, and he used his voice to cry out to God. We, too, must cry out to our Shepherd. Our Shepherd has thick skin, big shoulders, and plenty of time to listen. He longs to hear from you, from your heart. The Lord is not looking for plastic platitudes of praise but authentic cries of your heart. As you and I follow Jesus, we will pick up lots of dings and dents in this life. We must be real with our words to the Lord.

When was the last time you cried out to your Shepherd?

You must name it. Just as Jesus asked the demon in Luke 8:30, "What is your name?" we must name the things that have kept us in the dark valley. It's time for you to cry out to him. Find a quiet place and pour out your heart using this application activity.

Application Activity

Start journaling. Write out your thoughts, regardless of how troubling or embarrassing they may be. Often, when you see on paper what is going on in your head, you will be surprised by how much more manageable your problem becomes. Give no thought to grammar or spelling, just write. Move your thoughts onto paper.

2. David took a stand; you take a stand

When I am afraid,
*   I put my trust in you.*
For you have delivered my soul from death,
*   yes, my feet from falling,*
that I may walk before God
*   in the light of life.*

—Psalm 56:3, 13

David experienced the chaotic rush of depression and despair, the feeling of everything once nailed down in his life now coming loose. Men were after him, God was distant, time was closing in, and options were fading fast. Times of depression can feel like your feet are planted in midair. Circumstances seem like shifting sand, and you are in the middle of it, sinking fast. Something or someone must change.

The only person you can change is yourself. This is the time you must take a stand. This is the time you must find a firm foundation, something you can stand on, something you can trust in because it does not change.

The promises of God must become the foundation of your life. Dr. V. Raymond Edman said, "Never doubt in the dark what God has shown you in the light."[1] You have to stand on the Word of God. The Word is the lamp to our stumbling feet. We must anchor ourselves to the forged steel of the Scriptures. Since depression doesn't have an expiration date, we must trust in the power of the Word of God. The Word of God formed the universe. The Word of God must become your anchor, your rock, and your fortress when your feelings of despair are shouting in your ear.

It's time for you to take a stand. Find a quiet place and stand on the Word of God.

Application Activity

Write out encouraging Bible verses and tape them up in your house or at work, or carry them in your purse or wallet. Refer to them and memorize them whenever you are struggling with unhealthy thoughts. Turn on uplifting Christian music. Sing and meditate on the principles of God's Word. Praise and worship the Lord. By all means, turn off any music or television that saddens you or causes you to focus on your troubles. Here are some wonderful Scriptures on several vital topics.

Suffering: 1 Peter 4:12–16; Romans 8:17–18; 2 Corinthians 4:17; James 1:2–4

Forgiveness/Mercy: Hebrews 4:16; Matthew 18:21–22; Hebrews 8:12; Proverbs 11:19; James 5:9

Thankfulness: Philippians 4:11; Hebrews 13:5; I Thessalonians 5:18

Fear/Worry/Doubt: Matthew 6:25–34; Philippians 4:6–7; 2 Timothy 1:7; 1 Corinthians 10:13; Isaiah 41:10

3. David stepped forward; you step forward

Purge me with hyssop, and I shall be clean; wash me, and I shall be whiter than snow. Let me hear joy and gladness; let the bones that you have broken rejoice. Hide your face from my sins, and blot out all my iniquities. Create in me a clean heart, O God, and renew a right spirit within me. Cast me not away from your presence, and take not your Holy Spirit from me. Restore to me the joy of your salvation, and uphold me with a willing spirit.

—Psalm 51:7–12

Soren Kierkegaard, the German theologian, once said that life can only be understood when looking back, but we must live by looking forward. We also have a similar saying: "Hindsight is 20/20." David lived facing forward and looked back with understanding. This type of posture made him a man of repentance. David did not always make the best first decision, but he always seemed to come to his senses and repent. Then he made a good second decision.

We are not called to create a fantasy faith. David did not live in a fantasy. He owned his issues and stood as a sinner before the Lord. Much of the depression that David dealt with came from his personal sin. Never make peace with your personal sin. Wage holy war against it.

David was a man of repentance, and we will learn together that repentance is a salve to the hurts of the human soul. Moving forward means we must acknowledge our failures and sins, even if they are not the direct cause of our depression. Unconfessed sin hinders the work of the Spirit in our lives to bring healing and refreshment. To move forward like David, we must repent of the sins of our past. Don't squander future joy by holding onto past sins.

It's time for you to practice stepping forward. Find a quiet place and pour your heart out using this application activity.

Application Activity

Repentance requires honesty. No one comes to God with true repentance in their heart unless they've first acknowledged their need for forgiveness and reconciliation with him. Only those who have ceased trying to cover up their sin with self-righteousness and deceit can experience the profound and lasting change that comes only through repentance.

With honesty and sincerity, ask the Lord to reveal any and all sin in your life. Take the time to write a word down for each thing the Spirit of God brings to your mind. Don't rush this. Allow the Spirit of God to search your heart. After you have created a list of words that represent your sin, confess them to the Lord. Ask for his forgiveness. Request his cleansing touch on your heart, soul, and mind. Take the list and place it into a fire where you can watch your sin being cleansed as the fire incinerates those words. Your past is forgiven, your present is now, and your future is secured. It's time to journey forward.

I strongly encourage you to actually do the application activities I have suggested. When we're depressed, we often struggle with having adequate motivation, and we are weighed down by a sense of "this isn't going to make any difference." We have to *choose* against these things. The choices we make *do* make a difference—a huge one. We may not see that in 24 hours, but we will certainly see it over time.

Remember, seven days of good choices make a good week.

David truly does instruct us in the appropriate ways to walk through the valley. As we follow his lead, we need to remember this: we only have one real focus in all of our applications. Our focus is the Good Shepherd. He is the One who is going to lead us through. He is the One who is our strength. He is the One who, David discovered, can truly satisfy our souls. He is the One we can come to know more deeply and love more deeply, even when life is difficult or, often, *because* life is difficult.

In the following chapters, we are going to let our guide—David the shepherd boy, the mighty warrior, the king—help us know the Good Shepherd in a way we never really have before.

Now is not the time to give up.

Take another small step.

FOLLOW THE SHEPHERD

I find myself frequently depressed—perhaps more so than any other person here. And I find no better cure for that depression than to trust in the Lord with all my heart, and seek to realize afresh the power of the peace-speaking blood of Jesus, and His infinite love in dying upon the cross to put away all my transgressions.

—Charles Spurgeon

CHAPTER THREE

Faith in the Valley

Now faith is the assurance of things hoped for,
the conviction of things not seen.

—Hebrews 11:1

Do you believe you can walk through this valley? You may not, but faith says you can. This is not your death valley.

Death Valley National Park is one of the hottest, driest, lowest places on the planet. Its more than 3 million acres feature a diverse landscape that includes massive sand dunes, vast salt flats, rock formations, and canyons. An elevation of 282 feet below sea level makes it the lowest place in North America. Its two inches of annual rainfall make it the driest. An average July high temperature of 117 degrees makes it the hottest (its record high is 134 degrees on July 10, 1913). In 2001, Death Valley saw a record 153 consecutive days with daytime high temperatures above 100 degrees. But here is the fact that blows my mind: Even with its extremes, the park still receives nearly a million visitors each year.

Who are all these heat seekers?

In 1849, groups of pioneers with dollar signs in their eyes set off for California's gold fields. Hoping to find gold and achieve their dreams, some groups strayed into Death Valley as a shortcut to their destination. Think about walking a 120-mile basin. The average person can walk about 25 miles per day under good conditions. However, this basin provided anything but good conditions. The heat was scorching, the valley relentless. One group endured a two-month ordeal described as a nightmare of "hunger and thirst and an awful silence."[1]

Dehydration set in quickly. One person died. Others were rescued before they followed their friend to his desert grave. One of the last to leave turned around and looked down from a mountain at the narrow valley they had traversed. "Good-bye, Death Valley," he said, unknowingly naming the area.[2]

Some travelers through the hellish valley died, but others made it through. Why? As Winston Churchill said, "If you're going through hell, keep going." You will find that the key to survival is the practice of continuing.

Maybe this is your situation: You were on a journey to find gold—California-type gold in a friendship, marriage, business venture, move across the country, or new home. Off you went with best of intentions. At first the journey went fine. But as time passed, you realized you were nowhere near the gold. In fact, the journey was worse than just a missed opportunity; you found yourself in a valley. And this valley began to feel like a death valley of sorts. You quickly developed a hunger and thirst for relief and then felt that awful silence.

Not being prepared for a journey through Death Valley leaves you exposed in ways you never imagined. There is an overwhelming sense that you will die there. The clouds of depression begin to form in you. When you are in a death valley, every one of your senses is ambushed. Your life and death issue is not dehydration, but depression. Both take a toll on the human body and soul. You are alone, and frankly, you are scared.

Your fear is real. You were not prepared for the onslaught of extreme emotions, feelings, and thoughts. This is not just any valley; it is a death valley.

How do you do what Churchill advised? How do you keep going? Does a Christian have any unique supplies that can sustain him or her in a death valley? Yes, there is a reason for great hope. You have something that will get you through this, something that God loves to multiply and use for his glory and your good. Here is what you need during this time: faith. Jesus said with minuscule faith—that of a mustard seed—you can move mountains.

Before we even start the journey through Psalm 23, we need to make sure you understand the value of faith.

Mountain-moving faith is exactly what you need in a valley. You see, you don't have to have it all figured out to move forward because you can move forward in faith. Before you get any further into this book, you must get a handle on faith. Our faith rises and falls, yet faith is fuel for the fainthearted.

> **Our faith rises and falls, yet faith is fuel for the fainthearted.**

I like to think of faith as an acronym.

Focused **A**ttention **i**n **T**ruth and **H**ope

Faith is how you started your journey when you surrendered your life to Christ. Faith is what redeems your past and secures your future. Faith to the depressed Christian is what oxygen is to a person's lungs. Faith is going to get you through—not immediately out of—Death Valley. Faith can handle the heat while you are in the valley. It acts as a thermostat of the human soul. Let's break this faith thing down into small bites.

Focused attention in truth and hope

We do not believe *in* faith; we believe *with* faith. Faith by itself is not a stand-alone truth, but a tool that accesses truth. Everyone lives by faith. The object of your faith is what distinguishes you as a Christian. Faith is the grace tool that the Lord has given you for your Death Valley walk. This is crucial for understanding how to survive and even thrive in a Death Valley experience.

Faith in the valley is seeing the ultimate good over the immediate good. Faith in the valley makes that which is unseen visible to the heart and mind. Faith is taking the first step, even when God has not revealed the second step.

Most believers are permitted to go through emotional and spiritual valleys that are designed to test their faith in the crucible of fire. Why? Because faith ranks at the top of God's priorities. Without it, Hebrews 11:6 says, *"It is impossible to please him [God]."* And what is faith? It is, according to Hebrews 11:1 (KJV), *"The substance of things hoped for, the evidence of things not seen."* Pastor and author Dr. Tony Evans describes faith this way: "Faith is acting like something *is* so even when it is *not* so in order that it might *be* so simply because God *said* so."[3] You probably need to read that one again. If God says something is so, *it really is so,* regardless of whether it seems so right now to our senses. What God says is always more of a reality than what we see right now in front of our eyes. That's why the apostle Paul said:

> *We look not to the things that are seen*
> *but to the things that are unseen.*
> —2 Corinthians 4:18

> *We walk by faith, not by sight.*
> —2 Corinthians 5:7

Faith is the defiant "Nevertheless, God has said so." This determination to believe when visible proof is not provided and when our questions are not answered is central to our relationship with the Lord. He will never do anything to destroy our faith or the need for faith. Rather, he guides us through times of testing, specifically to cultivate this belief and dependence on him. This is so evident in Hebrews 11:7:

> *By faith Noah, being warned by God concerning events as yet unseen, in reverent fear constructed an ark for the saving of his household. By this he condemned the world and became an heir of the righteousness that comes by faith.*

Notice the ark was constructed by faith. Noah was guided and guarded by faith. Jewish tradition says that Noah planted tree seeds to grow trees to provide the wood. Noah took God at his word. And that trust lasted longer than a month, a year, or even a decade. For 120 years, he took God at his word and without the slightest change to his circumstances. 120 years! I would assume Noah had some long seasons of despair and discouragement. But he kept taking God at his word.

Where does doubt come from? It comes from the pit of hell. It comes from the liar. It comes from the thief. It comes from the bloodthirsty lion. It comes from the one whose mission statement, according to Jesus in John 10:10, is *"to steal and kill and destroy"* you and me. Satan's first move is to throw a wrench into the wheel of faith. Remember in Genesis 3:1 what he said to Eve in the garden as she held the fruit in her hand? "Did God say…not to eat that fruit?" Her faith in God was assaulted in that very moment. Eve began to doubt because of Satan rather than trust the certain word established by God. What are you going to choose today?

Remember that faith is a gift from God, according to Ephesians 2:8–9. God has given each of us a gift that gets us through the valley. Paul writes in Romans 12:3:

For by the grace given to me I say to everyone among you not to think of himself more highly than he ought to think, but to think with sober judgment, each according to the measure of faith that God has assigned.

In a death valley, your prayer may need to change. Instead of asking for a way out, what to do next, or how to fix the situation, you need to ask for more access to the faith God has already given you. You might say, "But I don't have that amount of faith." But you do. Peter writes in 2 Peter 1:3, *"His divine power has granted to us all things that pertain to life and godliness"* (emphasis added). Maybe you are like the father in Mark 9 who watched Jesus deliver an evil spirit from his son. In verse 24 he said to Jesus, "I believe; help my unbelief!" He needed more access to the gift of faith. Cry out to the Shepherd. He hears, he cares, and he will answer. Your bouts of melancholy can be the very moments of faith expansion.

The single greatest complaint that Jesus ever voiced about his disciples was their failures in faith. Over the course of his three-year ministry, again and again he said to them, "O you of little faith." His issue was not their absence of faith but their failure to exercise it and rest in it. It was a qualitative issue, not a quantitative issue. That is, it wasn't that they didn't have enough faith. Jesus taught them that they only needed faith the size of a mustard seed (the smallest of seeds). Rather, it was the quality of their faith. To put it more accurately, it was a matter of who their faith was in—themselves or Jesus.

Christ must be the object of our faith—not what can I do in the valley of depression or despair but what can Christ do?

For the disciples, faith expansion always happened in the heat of the valley—moments like watching the storm on the Sea of Galilee, seeing thousands of hungry people along the sea, standing at the graveside of Lazarus, or watching Jesus walking on water. Often, their faith wavered and was weak. We struggle with the same faith battle. But the level at which our faith is being exercised can change. That is growth. As pastor and author Mark Batterson writes, "Today's faith ceiling will become tomorrow's faith floor."[4]

> Christ must be the object of our faith—not what can I do in the valley of depression or despair but what can Christ do?

The great news about death-valley periods is that faith can be exponentially expanded during your trek through. You must understand that God is about the business of developing your belief in the midst of your despair. Faith expansion does not just come after the depression or heaviness lifts. No, it comes right here, right now. The Shepherd is increasing, expanding, stretching, and stoking your faith. Stop listening to the "oughts" and "shoulds" and allow the Shepherd to grow your faith. Remember, faith starts with "focused attention," which means faith starts in the mind. Like water, faith does not travel uphill but flows down from the head to the heart. Faith is born from a choice. Drop the "I can't" and replace it with "I will." Choose faith.

Again, the power of faith is not faith itself but the object in which it is placed. Placing your faith in the Creator of the universe is always a smart move. When you're lost in a deep, dark valley, bumper-sticker faith just does not work.

Try this with me. Stop for a moment and find a quiet place. Let's practice what the apostle Paul wrote in Philippians 4:8:

> Finally, brothers, whatever is true, whatever is honorable, whatever is just, whatever is pure, whatever is lovely, whatever is commendable, if there is any excellence, if there is anything worthy of praise, think about these things.

Take a moment. Set your mind on what God says is true, honorable, just, pure, lovely, commendable, excellent, and worthy of praise.

Did you do it? Did Jesus come to mind? If so, of course! He is all those things. Setting your mind on who Jesus is, what he has done, what he is doing, and what he will do naturally causes your faith to grow. Fixing your mind on Jesus starts fixing your mind.

The great miracle you need is not in your outer circumstances but in your mind. Getting through the valley requires many moments of stopping and thinking about what you know to be true about God, the object of your faith. You may never be able to change your circumstance, but you can change your thoughts.

You probably have heard of the phrase "paradigm shift." What we were just practicing could be called a "perspective shift." The change happens in the mind—changing your perspective from a focus on circumstances to focus your attention on the nature and character of God. Depression is not a choice for most, but perspective is a choice for all. Perspective is choosing to think with a biblical mindset.

The great news is that over time, small perspective shifts lead to a big paradigm shift. As we place our focus on God, he really does become bigger in our eyes than whatever we are facing, whether difficult outward circumstances or inner struggles. And that kind of perspective produces the fruit we long for—his peace in us, a peace that the world cannot give, a peace that, as Paul said, passes understanding.

James, the half brother of Jesus, wrote his New Testament book about tested faith. Remember, before the resurrection, James did not believe his brother was God; he believed his brother was nuts. You probably would have, too. What would your brother have to do to convince you that he was the eternal Son of God? Rise from the dead? Yep, that would make me a believer. It sure did make James a believer. So James knew firsthand what faith was because his faith was authentic faith.

James knew you could never have genuine faith until you had a tested faith. James 2:26 says, *"Faith apart from works is dead."* Our culture has a saying: "Actions speak louder than words." In other words, stop talking and start doing. You cannot have faith if it is not expressed. Faith is expressed when acted upon. Faith is acting like God is telling the truth. This type of faith is a verb in a Christian's life. If you are ready to "faith your depression" instead of "faking your happiness," you could be on the verge of a mini-breakthrough.

> **It's time to make faith a verb.**

It's time to make faith a verb.

Consider all you have to do to fake happy. Why not use the same amount of energy you use to fake happy and instead faith your depression? This is about making choices each morning. As God's mercies are new every morning, so your choices must be. Choose to rise. Choose to think biblically. Choose to serve others. Choose prayer. Choose Bible study. Choose church. Choose small group. Choose to eat, or to stop eating. Choose exercise. All of these choices are faith choices. In depression, mere intellectual faith will not help. You need to survive before you can thrive. You need a working faith. Faith is declaring that the only way through the valley is dependence on God. Faith is coming to an end of yourself and to the beginning of God. Faith is acting on the fact that God said so.

Focused attention in truth and hope

We must drop the anchor in truth.

Living with bouts of depression will mean you will have some bad days, and you will have some good days. And the level of both your peaks and your valleys will fluctuate. Often, the lower the valley, the higher the peak.

In geology, the ups and downs are called topography. God likes variety, so he didn't just place us on a flat planet. He placed us on one with mountains, hills, canyons, and valleys. This variety is one of the beautiful wonders of creation. G. K. Chesterton noted that we can see great things from the valley.[5] What, primarily, do we see? Peaks. You can't be in a valley without a peak nearby. Peaks and ridges create valleys.

Life for the Christian has highs and lows, too. Recognizing this is by no means meant to be dismissive of your pain. Instead, it is inviting you into a broader view of truth, one that provides hope. Listen to Spurgeon describe his ups and downs with depression: "I suppose some brethren neither have much elevation or depression. I could almost wish to share their peaceful life, for I am much tossed up and down, and although my joy is greater than the most of men, my depression of spirit is such as few can have any idea of."[6]

The life of Spurgeon is a great reminder that you can love Jesus and hate your life.

The apostle Paul experienced his own peaks and valleys. To the church in Corinth he passed along this peak of hope:

> *What no eye has seen, nor ear heard, nor the heart of man imagined, what God has prepared for those who love him.*
>
> —1 Corinthians 2:9

On the flip side, Paul later wrote of his valley to the same church:

> *For we do not want you to be unaware, brothers, of the affliction we experienced in Asia. For we were so utterly burdened beyond our strength that we despaired of life itself.*
>
> —2 Corinthians 1:8

At both points, however, Paul could declare, "For me to live is Christ" (Phil. 1:21). Paul embraced the beauty of life that is filled with peaks and valleys.

The truth is, there are meaning and purpose in the valley of depression. You can embrace this truth. I believe in you because I've seen many other people do it. When you do, you will begin to see the beauty of your life and the freshness of the Lord's grace.

Don't waste your valley. Your Death Valley journey is going to stretch both you and your faith. Does this mean that despair, discouragement, and depression are inconsequential? No, just the opposite. God is using the valley to increase something that is precious in the sight of God: your faith. Peter's first letter was written to Christians who were undergoing severe trials. To these Christians he said:

> *In this [their imperishable inheritance in Christ] you rejoice, though now for a little while, if necessary, you have been grieved by various trials, so that the tested genuineness of your faith—more precious than gold that perishes though it is tested by fire—may be found to result in praise and glory and honor at the revelation of Jesus Christ.*
>
> *—1 Peter 1:6–7*

The art of life is not flattening out your life's picture, but embracing the fact that life is comprised of peaks and valleys. Affliction is our brand. We must burn this truth into the fabric of our thinking. This book is going to help you learn to live and, yes, to love the topography of life. The full embrace of the Shepherd can only be found in accepting the combination of peaks and valleys. What if you could find both meaning and purpose in Death Valley? What if it becomes a reference point for the rest of your life?

Focused attention in truth and hope

Before we leave this chapter on Death Valley, let's finish with a focused hope about a valley. Put your airplane tray tables down; it's time to feed on hope. Remember the chick flick *Hope Floats*? I never saw it, but I love the title because hope does float when you are the one sinking. One attitude that depression hates is hope. The 18th-century English novelist George Eliot penned, "What we call despair is often only the painful eagerness of unfed hope."[7]

Hope is not a mystery. Winston Churchill once described Russia as "a riddle wrapped in a mystery inside an enigma." Hope can appear the same way to a Christian in depression. So let's start by answering the basic question: What is hope? The English language presents hope as a roll of the dice, things that might happen, by chance, if we are lucky enough. This kind of hope provides for a random life with high doses of chaos, full of empty calories of wishful promises.

There is a much better hope—a biblical hope that you can attach yourself to while you walk through the valley of depression. Should you miss this, the heat of the valley will not just singe your eyebrows but burn your skin. Hope must rise as the temperature of affliction rises. That is why hope means something entirely different in the Scriptures than in your dictionary.

When you read the word *hope* in the Bible, as in 1 Peter 1:13 (*"set your hope fully on the grace that will be brought to you at the revelation of Jesus Christ"*), it is not talking about wishful thinking. It's not "I don't know if it's going to happen, but I hope it happens." That's not what is meant by Christian hope. Christian hope is a conviction, a confidence that is born out of the Word of God. Biblical hope is when God has promised that something is going to happen, and you put your firm trust and expectation in his promise. Christian hope is a confidence that something will come to pass because God has promised it will come to pass. You hear hope in the voice of Job, *"Though he slay me, I will hope in him"* (Job 13:15). God does some of his best work in valleys when you choose to feed on hope. Valleys are perfecting because hope is life-giving. You can lose everything but hope and still get through the valley. G. K. Chesterton wrote, "Hope means hoping when things are hopeless, or it is no virtue at all....As long as matters are really hopeful, hope is mere flattery or platitude; it is only when everything is hopeless that hope begins to be a strength."[8]

Like faith, hope is a verb when you are in Death Valley. The author of Psalm 40 declares in no uncertain terms what hope does:

> *I waited patiently for the Lord;*
> *he inclined to me and heard my cry.*
> *He drew me up from the pit of destruction,*
> *out of the miry bog,*
> *and set my feet upon a rock,*
> *making my steps secure.*
> *He put a new song in my mouth,*
> *a song of praise to our God.*
> *Many will see and fear,*
> *and put their trust in the Lord.*
>
> —Psalm 40:1–3

Spurgeon talks about the disease of self-trust—the tendency to trust in ourselves when life goes well. This self-trust is really crooked-lumber thinking and leads to those dreadful four words: "I can handle it." It is so easy for us to trust in our common sense, prudence, and planning until we experience a severe shock, unexpected loss, or significant hardship. Then we see where we had placed our hope.

The action of hope is found in the first six words of Psalm 40: "I waited patiently for the Lord." Hope is actively waiting, not passively wanting. You might want circumstances to change or meds to kick in, or you may want to run away from everything around you. Consider putting those desires aside for the moment and instead actively waiting upon the Lord. Let hope change your wanting into waiting.

Hope does not rise from hollowed-out platitudes filled with whipped cream but from a patient trust in God. Paul described it this way in Colossians 1:27: "Christ in you, the hope of glory." Hope rises from the promise of heaven and eternity with the God who formed you and loves you. Though the book *Your Best Life Now* is a bestseller, we know the falsehood of this thinking. Hope teaches that our best life is in the life to come, and nothing can rob us of that life to come.

Hope declares that even though you have despair, you also have Christ, and best of all, Christ has you. Christian hope is a constant reminder that our best days are always in front of us. Heaven is coming and will last forever, and this season will pass. Hope is not just laying a current burden down, but it is also picking up God's promise for the future. There are hundreds of promises of God in the Scriptures. Feed hope with verses like these:

But you, O Lord, are a shield about me, my glory,
and the lifter of my head. I cried aloud to the Lord,
and he answered me from his holy hill. I lay down
and slept; I woke again, for the Lord sustained me.
I will not be afraid of many thousands of people
who have set themselves against me all around.

—Psalm 3:3–6

Because you are precious in my eyes, and honored,
and I love you, I give men in return for you,
peoples in exchange for your life. Fear not, for I
am with you; I will bring your offspring from the
east, and from the west I will gather you.

—Isaiah 43:4–5

For I am sure that neither death nor life, nor angels
nor rulers, nor things present nor things to come,
nor powers, nor height nor depth, nor anything
else in all creation, will be able to separate us from
the love of God in Christ Jesus our Lord.

—Romans 8:38–39

Hope floats. Depression is real—your own depression is real—but so are the promises of God. Your past and your present do not have to incarcerate your future. As I wrote in the first chapter, I say it again, a Christian's best days are always ahead.

Ask the Lord to help you not waste this season, but to glean from it everything he has in store for you. Remember, you may not be what you should be or what you can be, but you are not what you were. You were rescued, you were ransomed, you were redeemed, and you will be rewarded.

You've got to keep walking.

CHAPTER FOUR

You Have a Shepherd

The Lord is my shepherd.

—Psalm 23:1a

And so we begin.

Not long ago, I read a quote by Dr. Richard Leahy, a prominent psychologist, that rocked my world. He wrote, "The average high school kid today has the same level of anxiety as the average psychiatric patient in the early 1950s."[1] As we have noted, teens aren't the only age group suffering from anxiety or a host of other mental health issues such as depression. Far from it.

We live in a world that has become very stressed and very stretched. It's the big elephant in the room of our culture. It's even the elephant in the room in the church. The Christian culture in America is stressed and stretched. It's not something we talk about much, though. We'd rather turn on a football game or the latest Netflix series. We have a Shepherd we need to follow, not run ahead of and expect him to follow us because of our panic.

As we look at walking through the valley of discouragement, despair, or depression, we have chosen as our human guide a man who knew how to slow down and experience God's rest. We are going to camp out in David's most famous and incredibly rich psalm: Psalm 23. Listen again with fresh ears to the words of King David:

> *The LORD is my Shepherd; I shall not want.*
> *He makes me lie down in green pastures.*
> *He leads me beside still waters.*
> *He restores my soul.*
> *He leads me in paths of righteousness*
> *   for his name's sake.*
> *Even though I walk through the valley of the*
> *shadow of death,*
> *   I will fear no evil,*

for you are with me;
> *your rod and your staff,*
> *they comfort me.*
You prepare a table before me
> *in the presence of my enemies;*
you anoint my head with oil;
> *my cup overflows.*
Surely goodness and mercy shall follow me
> *all the days of my life,*
and I shall dwell in the house of the LORD
> *forever.*

When we think about this psalm, what usually comes to mind is all of its poetic and incredibly uplifting language. It's easy to overlook the very stark realities that David acknowledges we face:

- There is a place in life called the valley of the shadow of death.
- Evil is real and all around us.
- We have enemies.
- We are prone to wander into areas that are bad for us.
- Our souls have an ongoing need for inner rest.

That is just a short list of realities that David acknowledges in the psalm.

Fortunately, David, as God testified, was a man after God's own heart. He knew what it meant to walk deeply with God. And he knew that God was sufficient for all the difficulties we face, including stressed-out living and, yes, depression.

In a very real sense, Psalm 23 is God's antidote to, or vaccination for, depression and discouragement. Though it was penned a thousand years before Christ, the psalm can be considered an Old Testament foundation for Christian living. In it we find the truths, the principles, and the applications that we desperately need when we are going through desperate (or even not so desperate) times.

Most likely, David wrote this psalm while a civil war was being waged against him in Israel, an attempt to remove him from his throne and end his life. The worst part for David was that the rebellion was being led by David's own son Absalom. David was forced to flee to Jerusalem. When he wrote Psalm 23, he had probably reached Mahanaim, a town on the other side of the Jordan River. He was awaiting word as to how his troops had fared in an important battle.

So when David writes of the valley of the shadow of death, he wasn't speaking figuratively. His life truly was being threatened, just as it had been many times before.

The kingdom was torn in two, his own life threatened, his son leading the rebellion. If ever there was a time to be depressed, that was it, and David knew it. Yet, in the midst of it all, David penned this magnificent psalm, a blueprint for us journeying through times in our lives that weigh so heavily upon us.

In the following chapters, we are going to dive into the deep waters of the truths David unfolds. Each one is vital to us as we walk through difficult times.

God is our Shepherd

The first truth in the valley is perhaps the most vital of all. If we don't get it right, the rest of Psalm 23 won't make any sense. It will be just bumper-sticker theology. It could be said that the remainder of the psalm is simply David amplifying the very first truth he states.

To get the full impact of what David says first, we have to remember who David was. Before becoming king leading the Israelites in battle, serving King Saul at the palace, defeating Goliath, or being anointed by the prophet Samuel, David was a shepherd boy. He spent years on the hillsides, alone, tending the sheep. David knew sheep. He knew what they were like and everything they needed. He knew what it was to be a shepherd.

> We've got to get God in the right position.

So David starts by penning these words: "The Lord is my shepherd" (Ps. 23:1). The first thing David talks about in this psalm is the position that God has in his life. There's a reason David starts here. Nothing could be more critical in our lives. The very foundation of Christian living is this: *We've got to get God in the right position.* David declares what position God is in. He says, "The Lord is my shepherd."

> When in the valley of despair, the first act of your will must be to surrender your darkness and any sense of control to the Shepherd.

When in the valley of despair, the first act of your will must be to surrender your darkness and any sense of control to the Shepherd.

If you are prone to making resolutions, here is a great one. Maybe someone gave you this book for Christmas. Here's a great New Year's resolution: This year, God is going to be my Shepherd. Jesus Christ is going to be my Good Shepherd. This is not a "sort of" or "kind of" resolution. This is a firm conviction of the heart and mind. What a significant, life-changing truth!

Every word is important in this psalm. I'd like you to notice how David refers to his shepherd. He refers to him very personally. He doesn't use the generic word for God. He uses the personal, intimate name for God: Yawheh, or Jehovah. It's the name God uses when Moses asked him, "Whom shall I tell them has sent me?" God said, "Tell them I am has sent you" (Exodus 3:14).

Yahweh. I am that I am. That's what Yahweh means. It's the name God gives for himself. David says Yahweh, Jehovah (another rendering of the same word), is my God. Jehovah Jireh, the Lord my provider—he is my Shepherd.

What David is saying to us as he opens this psalm is this: If you want this One to be your Shepherd, you have to be in a relationship with him. If you want to deal with the stretched, stressed-out, depression-inducing culture we live in, you have to have a personal relationship with the Shepherd. You have to know him as your Shepherd. And when you do, he is both Savior and Lord of your life.

David doesn't refer to God here as the "Mighty One" or the "Holy One," although he is those, too. In calling him Shepherd, David is emphasizing that God is not distant, aloof, or unapproachable—not at all. David is saying something like this: "He is *my* Shepherd. I am on intimate terms with him."

I think an analogy from my own life captures a little of the sense of this. Sometimes someone will come up to me and, wanting to get my attention, say, "Reverend?" And I have to think for a second before I recognize that they're talking to me because I don't think of myself as a reverend. I feel like saying, "Reverend? I'm not a reverend. Reverends are old and crotchety and maybe a little mean. I'm Pastor Todd. Call me that. Or just Todd."

There was a movie not long ago called *Saving Mr. Banks* in which Tom Hanks played Walt Disney. One of the things I loved about the movie (among many other things) was that Walt Disney never wanted to be referred to as Mr. Disney. He wanted to be called Walt. Here was a man who influenced entertainment around the world more than anyone else in the 20th century, and he always said, "Call me Walt." He wanted to be on a first-name basis.

I love the fact that King David says, "I'm on a first-name basis with my Shepherd. His name is Yahweh. It's Jehovah Jireh." The only way you can be on a first-name basis with Almighty God is when Jesus Christ is your Lord. He doesn't make himself available as Shepherd any other way.

This means first that we have entered into a personal relationship with this Shepherd through faith in his Son, Jesus Christ. The Shepherd sent his own Son to be our sacrificial lamb, to die on the cross for our sins—our sins, personally—and to rise from the dead to give us new, eternal life. God is only the Shepherd to those in his flock (John 10:1–16). We are brought into his flock when we personally choose to put our personal faith in the death and resurrection of his Son for us (Rom. 10:9–10).

Second, it means we embrace Jesus Christ each day as our own Shepherd, the one who leads us. That means *following* the Shepherd. There's no such thing as having Jesus Christ as your Shepherd unless you choose to be led and are willing to follow.

The truth is that we all follow someone. We deceive ourselves into thinking we don't, but we all do. We follow what entertainers tell us. We follow sports figures. We follow life coaches. We follow people on Twitter and Instagram (literally!). Or we simply follow what our culture tells us is important. Some of us follow our kids. We think they're following us, but it's actually the other way around.

So we all follow someone. Unfortunately, some of the people we follow are nuts. I live in California, so trust me, I see people following the crazies every day. And even if they aren't, no one and no culture on this planet can be a good shepherd to us. No one can know exactly the care we need or the path we need to take. Only God knows

> **A SIDE NOTE TO PARENTS:** Shepherd your kids. They can't shepherd themselves. How do we do that? Start by giving them a high view of God. Teach them and show them by your life that he is Lord. When they have a high view of God, they will be ready to let him shepherd them.

that. Some of our discouragement and depression comes from placing our eyes on the wrong target.

I love how David, the all-powerful king of Israel, at whose word people lived or died, who got whatever he wanted whenever he wanted, says with all humility, "I have a Shepherd. I follow Yahweh. I trust him."

This is the thing about following your Shepherd. Either you are following him, or you aren't. You can't be a kind-of follower. You can't say, "I'm kind of following Jesus today." It doesn't work that way. It's like being pregnant. My wife, Stacey, was pregnant three times. And she never came up to me and said, "Todd, you won't believe this, but I'm kind of pregnant." You're either pregnant, or you're not. You're either letting Jesus be your Shepherd, or you're not.

Remember when Jesus said, "Seek ye third the kingdom of God?" Maybe you don't, because he never said it. He said, "Seek first the kingdom of God" (Matt. 6:33). Remember the first commandment God gave to Moses? "You shall have few other gods before me." Nope, not exactly. Nor did Jesus say, "Love the Lord your God with 50 percent of your heart, soul, mind, and strength."

The very foundation of Christian living is getting God in the right position in our lives. Once he is in the right position, we will have the right posture before him. Jesus is Lord. As we acknowledge him as Lord, we are ready to let him lead us as our Shepherd.

We are sheep

If the Lord is our Shepherd, what does that imply about us? This isn't a trick question. The implication is that we are sheep. God refers to his people as sheep over 200 times in the Bible.

David knew something about sheep. He had certainly spent enough time caring for them. So he knew what he was talking about when he said that God was the Shepherd and we are the sheep.

Sheep are timid. They are fearful. They panic easily. They are easily frustrated. They are dumb and gullible. They are vulnerable to pests and hunger. They are easily influenced by a leader. They stampede easily, being vulnerable to the mob mentality. They have little or no means of self-defense; they can only run, and they aren't extremely fast, so their enemies can kill them easily. Sheep are jealous and competitive for dominance. They constantly need fresh food, have little discernment, and are stubborn, insisting on their own way. They are easily flipped over on their backs, unable to right themselves. They can die of starvation if somebody doesn't turn them back over. They are frequently looking for easy places to rest. They don't like to be sheared or cleaned, and they are creatures of habit, getting into ruts.

There's a reason God refers to us as sheep.

For our purposes, what are some specific characteristics of sheep that we need to keep in mind as we see what David says about our Shepherd?

Stupid

First, sheep are *stupid*. Case in point: Have you ever seen trained sheep at the circus? Nope, and there is a reason for that. God must laugh at us sometimes, seeing the stunts we do that look pretty silly to everyone but us. A couple of years ago, the Smith family (that's me, my wife and kids, not some hypothetical family named Smith!) went to San Francisco. I had always wanted to visit a foreign country. While there, we visited Ripley's Believe It or Not Museum. It was awesome—weird, but awesome. You walk into the first room in the museum and see a crazy mirror that distorts you into all different shapes. It's set up to play a game where you look into the mirror and try to get your bottom lip to touch your nose. They showed this guy who could actually touch his nose with his bottom lip. So you contort your face, trying to duplicate him while looking at yourself in the mirror. Sounds silly, but it's really fun.

We did the mirror thing for a while, and then we went through the rest of the museum. At the end of the exhibits, we went into a room and instantly realized that the weird mirror in the first exhibit was actually a two-way mirror. Now we were on the other side of the mirror, watching all the people do ridiculous things with their lips. Once we got over the horror of what we had looked like, we watched the people on the other side. It was hilarious. I imagine God looks at us that way sometimes. We look and behave foolishly at times because we are sheep. We do dumb things.

The reason we need a shepherd to lead us is that we're not smart enough to lead ourselves. I'm not talking about intelligence here. I'm talking wisdom. Sometimes we are inclined to think, "I don't need a shepherd. I can make it down this hillside and up the next one just fine." Trust me, you need a shepherd. I need a shepherd. We all need a shepherd. We need someone to tell us no. We need someone to tell us go. We need someone to tell us to stop and rest. We need someone who can say, "I created you, and I know what's best." Only one Shepherd can say that.

> **Stop trusting yourself, and start trusting him. Don't be foolish.**

Stop trusting yourself, and start trusting him. Don't be foolish.

We especially need someone who knows us inside and out when we are depressed. When we suffer from depression, we often feel as if no one understands the depths of what we are dealing with. Often, we simply give up trying to help people understand. It's just not worth it. But there is One who understands perfectly.

Stained

Second, sheep are *stained*. If you do any study of sheep, you'll notice something about them. Sheep can't clean themselves.

Other animals can. In fact, God has created most other animals so they clean themselves. I'm a dog person. I love how when you come home at the end of the day, a dog will run up to you, lick you all over your face, and say as loudly as possibly, "I missed you all day!" Cats? Not so much. Cats are really just uncircumcised Philistines. You walk through the door, and they simply look at you, saying, "Hmmm. You're home? Well, whatever." Then they go back to doing what they've been doing most of the day, which is picking at their paws, licking their fur—cleaning themselves. Animals clean themselves. Did you know giraffes have a 20-inch tongue that they use to clean their own ears? Try that one at a dinner party!

But sheep? Nothing. They can't keep themselves from getting dirty, and once they are, they can't do anything about it. They need a shepherd to clean them.

We are sheep. We get ourselves dirty, and we can't clean ourselves. We dwell on wrong thoughts, we harbor wrong attitudes, and we do sinful things. All of these things stain us on the inside, and we can't clean ourselves up. We need a shepherd.

That's why the Great Shepherd, through the prophet Isaiah, said, "Though your sins are like scarlet, they shall be as white as snow" (Isa. 1:18). Jesus came to "take away sins" (1 John 3:5), and that's exactly what he did at the cross. John says that "if we walk in the light, as he is in the light…the blood of Jesus his Son cleanses us from all sin" (1 John 1:7). In other words, when we let God be our Shepherd, he cleans us up. No sin is too messy for him. He cleans up not only the individual sins, but whole patterns of thinking and behaving. He changes us into the image of his Son, according to Paul in Romans 8:29:

> For those whom he foreknew he also predestined to be conformed to the image of his Son, in order that he might be the firstborn among many brothers.

It's what he's good at.

Stubborn

Third, sheep are *stubborn*. Despite the fact that they can't take care of themselves and are completely dependent on someone else to do it for them, they don't want to be told what to do. Doesn't make much sense, does it? But no one ever accused sheep of making much sense.

When being gathered, sheep at times will simply refuse to cooperate. The stubborn sheep have to be chased, taken down like a calf being roped, and carried to where they need to go. When on a rope, sheep often don't want to be led. They will pull against the rope, and sheep can pull hard. The stubbornness of sheep is fully seen when it comes to being sheared. This is when their iron will is clearly evident.

Well, once again, we are like sheep. We like things our own way. We are like the person James warns of in his epistle. We look at what God says in his Word like we're looking at ourselves in a mirror. Then we walk away from the mirror and forget what we looked like (James 1:23–24). We forget (or ignore) what God just told us. We think we know better, and we want to do it our own way. My heart breaks when I see people sitting in our church week after week, listening to the teaching of God's Word, and then they go out and do the exact opposite of what God says to do. They end up in the office of one of the pastors on our staff, their lives in shambles.

If your life is in shambles, or if you just feel like your life is in shambles (which is what depression does to us), there is good news. It's never too late to say to God that we need him to be our Shepherd. We've always needed him to be our Shepherd; we just didn't always admit it to ourselves. And when we do, he will lead us. The places he leads, David tells us, are good. Very good.

Remember, Jesus never ran anywhere.

Start behind the Shepherd.

TRUST THE SHEPHERD

Before any great achievement, some measure of depression is very usual.

—Charles Spurgeon

CHAPTER FIVE

Dealing with Life's Wants

I shall not want.

—Psalm 23:1b

A few years back, the Spice Girls, a British pop group, produced a song called "Wannabe." Its opening lyrics went like this:

Yo, I'll tell you what I want, what I really really want,
So tell me what you want, what you really really want,
I'll tell you what I want, what I really really want,
So tell me what you want, what you really really want,
I wanna, I wanna, I wanna, I wanna, I wanna really
really really wanna zigazig ha.

The lyrics didn't go any deeper as the song progressed. The height of British cultural achievement it was not. But the lyrics do capture the essence of the human condition. We want. We want this. We want that. We want *everything*.

First, we want a spouse; then we want a better spouse. We want kids; then we want better kids.

We want a better job, a better boss, better coworkers, and better customers.

We want a higher salary, more money in the bank, and a bigger IRA.

We want a better house, a better yard, a better TV, and maybe an entire home theater.

We want a better car, a better vacation, a better commute time, better seats at the football game, and a better golf swing.

We want a better church, a better pastor (Ouch! That hurts!), and a better Bible study group.

We want out of the valley right here and right now.

We want. We want. We really really want. It never ends!

David knew the human condition. He knew his own heart. He knew his tendency toward depression when he didn't get what he wanted. So after acknowledging that

God is his Shepherd, David said, "I shall not want." This declaration of faith in God's sufficiency was a safeguard against depression or at least a diagnostic of what might be wrong.

Imagine for a moment what it would feel like to be satisfied rather than always wanting more. That 1997 Volvo station wagon with 370,000 miles on it that still starts up fine? Good enough. That 1,600-square-foot, 45-year-old house with the closets packed to the brim? Good enough. That spouse who doesn't satisfy you in every way and fulfill all your needs? Good enough. Those kids who make B's and want to play video games too often and aren't perfect 100 percent of the time? Good enough. That vacation to Grandma's in Iowa when you really want to go to Hawaii? Good enough.

Facing life's wants

David writes in Psalm 23:1, *"The Lord is my shepherd; I shall not want."* In other words, Jesus satisfies; he is enough.

This is a soul-piercing question. If the darkness never lifts, is Jesus enough?

How does finding satisfaction in Jesus help with depression? It helps because so

> **This is a soul-piercing question. If the darkness never lifts, is Jesus enough?**

much of the undercurrent of depression really boils down to this: we aren't satisfied. We want. We want more. We want something different. We aren't happy with what God has provided for us, and that gets us depressed.

Not all depression arises from our unsatisfied wants, of course. Some depression has organic causes; that is, some depression is due to our bodies not producing the right balance of chemicals for normal emotional functioning. That's a medical issue that needs to be treated as a medical issue, and fortunately there are medications to help with such depression.

Frequently, depression is a response to painful difficult major life events. Divorce or the loss of a relationship can cause depression. That is normal. It takes time to recover from the severing of a relationship that you expected to be long-term, or for life. The death of a loved one falls into this category. So does major trauma. If you get in a car accident and lose both legs, you are probably going to get depressed. On the bright side, studies indicate that even after a major life trauma such as this, people, on average, return to their normal baseline emotional state within about a year. The flip side is also true; people who win the lottery are ecstatic at first and remain happier than normal for about a year. After that, they return to their baseline, pre-lottery emotional state.

I'm not saying it's inherently wrong to want things. I'm not saying it's wrong to prefer a Ford 150 pickup to that little 1980 Toyota pickup that can barely carry two bags of groceries. What we're really talking about here is *contentment*. Paul said, "*I have learned in whatever situation I am to be content*" (Phil. 4:11). Have we? If not, that's a great place to start when we are struggling with depression.

Learning to be content can be a battle, especially when depressed. It can take time. Sure, we all want to be out of the valley as soon as possible, but we must realize it may not be a quick fix, and we may have to find a level of contentment in the midst of walking through the valley. Remember, the apostle Paul prayed three times to have his thorn removed from his life. He wanted something, and that was the removal of the thing that constantly plagued him. The answer God gave him was to be content.

When David says, "I shall not want," he's saying that God provides what he needs. He wasn't looking to the people and things in the world to provide him with what they are not designed to provide: true fulfillment in life.

How many times do we have to learn the same lesson? We pursue something, we get it, and then we discover that it doesn't actually satisfy. It never does. This is a high-carb, low-protein lifestyle, and it leaves you wanting more. In the meantime, we tend to drift off course from what God intends for us.

Think with me for a moment about how pursuing some desires has been disastrous in people's lives. I know it has for me. How many times have I gotten myself in a bad predicament because I had a desire in my life that I thought I had to have fulfilled? I looked over and said, "The grass is greener over there. I love the grass over there. I want that grass."

The problem is that it's fake grass. But I don't know that until I get over in the other field and say to myself, "This isn't very satisfying." Or I get over into the field, and the grass really is greener. But you know why it's greener? Because it's got a massive watering bill. When I discover that, I don't want it anymore. But now that I'm in that field, I have to live with it.

David says something like this to us: "You have to get your wants under control, and if you put God in the right position, your wants will lose their power over you."

The seven seductions

This world offers almost unlimited opportunities to place our wants ahead of following the Shepherd. Instead of following the Shepherd, we substitute one of these wants to mask or numb our feelings. I want to highlight seven of them. I call them the seven seductions.

Situation: We want the past or the future, just not the present. Yet we can only live in one place—today. The past is over. The future has not happened, so just do today.

Status: We want to achieve success in the eyes of the world and have the perks that come with achieving in the sight of the world. We must realize that Christ will put the final price tag on everything, and we can stop chasing an empty-calorie status of this world.

Stuff: We want money and the things it can buy, whether material goods (literal stuff) or experiences (pleasurable times such as vacations or other experiences that may enrich our lives, such as education). Things can never satisfy the soul. Wealth is found in the stuff the Shepherd offers. Some people are so poor that all they have is money.

Security: We want assurance that our future and the future of those we love are taken care of. We want enough savings or possessions or a high enough income stream to have that assurance. The only thing in this life that is secure is our salvation, because the Lord guards it for us.

Significance: We want to feel like we have made a difference. Wanting to make a difference can be a positive if properly directed. If we are buying into what the world regards as making a difference, however, it can become an idol. Stop chasing a business card title. The people we seek to impress at work will show up at our funeral if it is at a convenient time for them. That is truth!

Substance: Food. Alcohol. Drugs. Tobacco. So many of us constantly seek what we can put into our bodies to make us feel a certain way. Substance-seeking has become the quicksand of life in America. Substances may provide a kick, but they come with a massive kickback.

Sex: We take what God designed for the expression of love, the experience of pleasure in marriage and for producing a family, and make it into an idol— something we can't live without. We know our bodies produce all kinds of chemicals during sex, which can be sought to soothe our pain, but they only lead to another level of hurt and bondage when pursued in ways contrary to God's will.

When we do not have what we want or if we have pursued these wants ahead of pursuing God, we frequently end up in a place we don't want to be: mired in depression and muddied with despair. For only the Shepherd, not the seductive seven, can fill the void we feel.

How are you doing?

Let's take a minute and explore these seven substitutes in our lives. The real question each of us has to face is this: Is Jesus Christ enough for you? That's where the rubber really hits the road. Is he enough? Or do we need some of Jesus and some of all the things this world has to offer to give our lives meaning? In the words of Saint Augustine, "Christ is not valued at all unless he is valued above all." Is Jesus enough for us?

My wife's voice and the voice of the Holy Spirit sound exactly the same. She has a small irritating 3x5 card that she keeps out and visible for all to see. On this card it says,

"If all you get in this life is Jesus, then your life has been a total success." Just like ET, I point to my chest and say "ouch."

I find it interesting that the word David used in Psalm 23 for "want" is the Hebrew word *khaw-sare*. We often think of wants as materialistic, and *khaw-sare* can refer to something material. But it has a broader meaning. It refers to all the areas of desire, including the seven mentioned above that we are so susceptible to wanting in unhealthy ways. By using the word here, it's as if David is saying to us, "Here's the deal. You've got to get God in the right position. When you do, you get your wants under control. You are going to be satisfied in him."

Lack of contentment can't be underestimated in our dark valleys. *Khaw-sare* speaks directly to the issue of status and what the people around us deem important. It confronts us with this question: Am I satisfied with where I am in my life right now? Am I satisfied just being a child of the King with the hope of heaven in front of me? David is saying something like this: "I am completely satisfied with that. I'm his. I'm very satisfied to wear the brand of God-follower." Today, he would phrase it, "I'm very satisfied in wearing the brand of Christ-follower.

David knew about branding sheep. Sheep aren't branded like cows are. The Shepherd would take a knife and cut the sheep's ear in a particular shape, a triangle or a square or a certain marking. That brand, that cut, was the symbol of that sheep being the shepherd's.

The world literally puts its brand on us. Brands are a big deal in our culture. You've got to have the right brands. If you're a kid growing up, you'd better be wearing the cool brands, not jeans and tennis shoes from a discount store. It's almost a matter of social life and death.

But we get older and grow out of that, right? Not quite. Ever want an Apple computer? An iPhone? A BMW? A Honda or Toyota instead of a Hyundai?

Well, it's a matter of quality, we say. Okay, fine. Ever buy a shirt with a logo on it that added $10 to the price? Was that really a matter of quality? I used to love Lacoste shirts—you know, the ones with the alligator on them. I was so cheap that when my Lacoste shirts got too old, I'd cut the alligator off and sew it onto my new generic shirts. I had to make it look Lacoste. Boy, confession feels so good.

The world wants to shape us into its brand. Instead, the brand we need to wear is this: We are satisfied being his. This is what author John Piper was getting at when he wrote, "God is most gloried in me when I am most satisfied in him."[1] Piper referred to this as Christian Hedonism, and it means finding ultimate pleasure in the Shepherd.

If for no other reason than we need to stop hiding, some of us need to raise the flag at work, at school, or wherever we are regularly with other people and say, "You know what? I'm a Christ-follower. I love and follow Jesus Christ. I'm his. He's my Shepherd." That's a big challenge for some of us. It really is. It's a statement of status, and it's also a statement of contentment. We must learn to be content. We must choose to be content.

The American economy runs on discontentedness. The goal of every marketing campaign is to make you discontent with what you have. How many families have been destroyed by this manufactured discontentedness? Maybe this is part of your valley experience right now. People run up massive debt, thinking that whatever they purchase will fulfill them. They are trying to keep up with the Joneses. What they don't realize is that the Joneses are in massive debt, too, and their family is falling apart because of the stress. Discontentedness does not help with depression and discouragement. It only adds fuel to the fire.

A few years ago, we bought a brand new TV. It was big. It was nice. After we bought it, I went into Best Buy to get something. I made my way to the back of the store and wandered into never-never land. It was a room with a home entertainment center, including a big reclining couch system, surround sound, a huge 3D TV screen, the works. So I kicked back and started watching a movie, and it was awesome. I sat there for a long time. Finally, I asked an employee, "If I move this whole system into my house, how much will it cost me?" He said, "$10,000." My first thought was to call Stacey, my wife, and say, "We are selling the kids on eBay."

You know what's so funny? When I first walked into the store, I was completely content with the TV we already had. It wasn't until I was faced with what I didn't have that I felt discontent.

That's one of the prime strategies of the enemy of our souls. He is the father of lies. He lies to us and says, "If you just get this…if you just had this…if you just…" He even whispers to us that if we can't stop being depressed, we can't follow Christ. This discontentment and hopelessness we feel is the slippery slope to the seven seductions. We would rather mask the pain, which is a symptom of our misplaced trust that things can make us happy, than to treat the disease with the Savior's grace.

The truth is that there is only one thing we can count on having: Jesus Christ. Everything else will eventually pass out of our lives. *Until we realize that Christ is the only thing we truly have, we will never realize that he's the only thing we truly need.*

Wants or needs?

You must be able to tell the difference between a want and a need. Paul wrote in Philippians 4:19, "My God will supply every need of yours." David said, "I shall not want" (Ps. 23:1). We need to ask ourselves if the things we are thinking about are wants or needs.

Psalm 23 is written from the perspective of the sheep. What does a sheep need? A sheep needs two things: protection and provision. That's it. Protect me and provide for me. That's all we really need. God's promise, which we can take to the bank, is that he will provide those two things every time. Will he provide them early? No, sometimes they'll come at the very last minute. Just ask the Israelites who left Egypt. But his promise is that he will provide. That's what he does for those who take him as their Shepherd.

We'll get nowhere in life without God being our Shepherd. We may make it to the corner office in our company, but it's still true: we'll get nowhere in life without God being our Shepherd. That means we'll get nowhere in life without Jesus Christ being our Lord. The goal is not just to get out of depression but to follow the Shepherd out of the valley and beyond.

Jesus, the Good Shepherd

Jesus didn't say, "I am the okay Shepherd." He said, "I am the Good Shepherd." He is really big on his name. He protects his name. He is a good Shepherd. Therefore, he will act as a good shepherd. He will take care of his sheep.

You may feel broken right now. Your world may feel shattered. You may feel out of control. In these times, we have to open our ears to what God says is true. He can handle our problems. He is the Good Shepherd. He can handle our fears. He's got us in his hands. Don't chase after the seven seductions. They will never satisfy your soul.

One day I was preparing a Sunday sermon, and I decided to use a snow globe—the ones kids like—to make a point. God has the whole world in his hands. I needed to take the bottom off (or so I thought) to make the point, but I couldn't get it off. So I got a small saw and sawed off the wooden base. When I reached a certain point, of course, the bottom came loose, and all the water and the "snow" came out. And I thought, *Well, there goes my point; the world is broken.*

But then it occurred to me, *this makes my point perfectly. Our world is broken. It's a wonderful creation, but it's broken. It needs someone to fix it.*

Our lives are like that. They are broken, often resulting in depression. We need someone to put our lives back together.

I love Psalm 95:4. It says the earth is in the Lord's hand. The broken earth is in his hand. You know what? Our individual lives are in his hands, too. Our families are in his hands. The Good Shepherd's hands carry us on.

He is our Shepherd. Because he is our Shepherd, we don't have to want. We can be satisfied with Christ.

He really is enough.

Keep on moving.

CHAPTER SIX

Rest Is Not a Dirty Word

He makes me lie down in green pastures.

—Psalm 23:2a

You have to slow down if you are going to go far.

I could've gotten rich. After graduating from high school long ago, I could've made a fortune if I had just realized that people would pay good money for energy. I don't mean energy for their homes or cars. I mean energy for themselves, for their bodies. Americans spend $15 billion per year on energy drinks, not to mention energy bars, energy pills, energy powders—you name it.

You have to ask yourself, what kind of a society spends tens of billions of dollars to pep itself up? The answer is a society that is exhausted. In an interview with *The Atlantic*, Brigid Schulte, author of *Overwhelmed: How to Work, Love, and Play When No One Has the Time*, spelled out the problem for us:

> We're working more hours—more extreme hours at one job at the upper end of the socio-economic spectrum and cobbling together several jobs to try to make ends meet at the lower end. Our standards for what it takes to be a good parent...are insanely high and out of proportion to all reality....We all feel like we're not doing enough for our children, so in our guilt, we do, do, do, and overdo: more lessons, more teams, more sports, bigger birthday parties, more educational outings.[1]

For women, she said:

> You have to keep house like Martha Stewart, parent like Donna Reed, work like

Sheryl Sandberg, and look like Jennifer Aniston. That's nuts. We all know it's nuts, and yet it's hard to break away from those cultural expectations. I soon discovered that men are beginning to feel as much or more overwhelmed than women, now that so many no longer just want to be the distant provider father, or just the fun dad or helper parent, but truly involved at home. They're doing now what women did 30 years ago—giving up time for sleep and personal care and spending almost all their "leisure" time with their kids. And I discovered...the constant dings and pings of technology and a new cultural value of busyness is now ramping the feeling of overwhelm for everyone.[2]

We're overcommitted, we're overworked, we're overbooked, we're overwhelmed. We are just flat-footed tired.

Another question: What kind of a society has tens of millions of people who are depressed? Answer: A society that is exhausted.

Americans are exhausted, and Americans are depressed. That isn't a coincidence. When we're depressed, it doesn't seem

> "And I discovered...the constant dings and pings of technology and a new cultural value of busyness is now ramping the feeling of overwhelm for everyone."

like the cause could be that we're simply worn out. Surely, we think, there are other, deeper issues than that. And there may well be. But exhaustion of both our bodies and our souls is a real contributor to despair and depression, and it exacerbates depression that may have arisen from other sources.

If we are followers of Jesus Christ, we have great hope for experiencing renewal rather than exhaustion. We have a Good Shepherd who knows how to replenish us. In Psalm 23, David wrote that there are three things God does as our Shepherd when we are exhausted and in need of rest and rejuvenation.

We're not talking about what God does for the lazy. To them, God says to stop being lazy (see Proverbs on that). No, we're talking about what God does for the exhausted. How does God treat worn-out, weary sheep?

He gives them the restorative rest and care they need. In a beautiful economy of words, he promises a wealth of soul-healing renewal.

> *He makes me lie down in green pastures.*
> *He leads me beside still waters.*
> *He restores my soul.*
>
> —Psalm 23:2–3a

When Jesus is your Lord and Savior, he is also your Good Shepherd, and he does three things for tired sheep: he makes, he leads, and he restores.

We will address the first one in this chapter and cover the next two in the following two chapters.

He makes

What is the first thing the Good Shepherd does? He makes us lie down in green pastures. He doesn't invite us to lie down. He doesn't say, "When you find the time, I'd love to meet you in that green pasture." No, he's the

Good Shepherd, and he makes us lie down.

If you study sheep, you will find that they are restless creatures. In fact, sheep need regular rest. Philip Keller, in his masterful book on Psalm 23, notes that a sheep will not lie down unless he or she is free from four things. Sheep have to be free from fear, they have to be free from conflict, they have to be free from pests, and they have to be free from hunger.[3] Then they will lie down. But the reality is that sheep never are free from those four things. So the shepherd actually has to make the sheep lie down in green pastures.

Sheep are restless by nature. There's a restless agitation to their lives. We are restless creatures as well. We're often agitated because we're looking for something better or worrying about what is next. We're always wanting to see the other field where it's a little bit greener. Combine our restlessness with the fact that we're embarrassed by the fact that we get tired, and you've got a recipe for exhaustion. We don't even like the fact that we need to sleep. Someone calls at 3:00 a.m.; we barely wake up and fumble around in the dark in time to answer it.

"Oh, I'm sorry, were you sleeping?"

"Me? No, not at all. Doing Bible study. So glad you called. How can I pray for you?"

The godly mathematician Blaise Pascal wrote, "I have often said that the sole cause of man's unhappiness is that he does not know how to stay quietly in his room."[4] We have a hard time practicing what Psalm 46:10 tells us to do: *"Be still, and know that I am God."* Our internal unrest wears us out.

The Good Shepherd sees this restless agitation in our lives and graciously makes us lie down. He knows that in our immaturity we won't choose to lie down.

It's like when you have little kids, and it's 7:00 or 8:00 in the evening. Little Johnny is crying, and you know it's been a day full of activity and he needs to go to bed. And Johnny says, "I'm not tired. I don't need any sleep. I could stay up all night!" So what do you do? Do you say, "Oh, all right. You can stay up until midnight"? No! You take him by the hand, lead him to the bed, lay him down, turn off the lights, tell him a story or sing him a song, and calmly sit. And in a matter of minutes, the little lamb that didn't need any rest is sound asleep.

As a parent, you are a good shepherd to your children. You make them lie down. Our Good Shepherd Jesus Christ does the exact same thing for us. He makes us lie down so we can find rest.

Unfortunately, we often fight this need for rest. We can be like kids who keep getting up for a drink of water. We just won't stay down. Keller notes that there are some sheep that just don't want to lie down. They want to go further. They want to explore the next field.

The Lord may be telling us to slow down and cut some things out of our lives, and we may be immature sheep who fight it. But we can only fight it for so long. He's the Good Shepherd, and he doesn't invite us to lie down—he makes us lie down. Either we take a pause in life, or God will make us take a pause.

A few years ago I started to have some physical problems. I had been running hard (as a lifestyle, not as an athlete) for years, and people were telling me to slow down. I kept saying, "No, no, no, I'm fine." I was burning the candle at both ends and in the middle. One Wednesday, I felt awful. I kept feeling awful on Thursday.

By Friday, I told my wife, Stacey, "Something is wrong, I feel really sick." By Saturday, I was in the ER, which I had fought against, too. I kept thinking, "I've got to keep going. People are counting on me."

My Good Shepherd made me lie down in that ER room where, after the CT scan, I found out I had pancreatitis. The doctor informed me that pancreatitis meant my pancreas was inflamed. And I thought, "What exactly is my pancreas? And how quickly can you remove it?"

So I went to that renowned medical journal where all the deep wealth of medical knowledge is stored — Google — and found out what a pancreas is and what pancreatitis is. It definitely wasn't something I wanted.

What I wanted was to be out of that hospital room as quickly as possible, but the Lord put me in there for six days. No food, just an IV. On the last day, when I was hoping to go home, I was still feeling really badly. The hospital chaplain came into my room and asked me if she could pray for me. She closed her eyes, and the second she said, "Dear Lord," I started weeping. I didn't stop crying, even after she said amen. I wept like a baby.

I remember thinking, "Lord, you've got this wrong. I'm supposed to be standing next to the bed, and I'm supposed to be praying for the person in the bed. This isn't right." And it was as if God said to me, "You know what, Todd? It's time to lie down. You haven't done it for years, so guess what I am doing? I'm the Good Shepherd, and I'm making you lie down."

I had bought into the spiritualized lie that it's better to burn out for Jesus than to rust out. So I just kept going and going and going until I crashed. I had to discover the hard way that burned out people aren't useful to the King at all. He had to make me lie down in order to finally get that. It took me about a year to get back to full health.

You may be running right now when you should be walking. Are you trying to run from your depression? The harder you try and the faster you run, the more exhausted you'll become.

So where does God make us lie down? In green pastures. I used to think of three things when I thought of green pastures: Maui, money, and shopping malls. Hey, God, you want me to lie down on the beach in Maui? Yeah, I'll suffer there. I'll go there. I'll even do it without lots of money. But if I have to lie down in a shopping mall (metaphorically), I'll have to have some cash.

Maybe we don't think of Maui or money or malls. Maybe we naturally picture a place like Ireland. We picture Ireland and think of hills and valleys and lush green pastures. We imagine the pastures there are so lush green that you can barely find the ground because the grass is so thick.

But have you ever been to Israel, where David penned Psalm 23? It's not Ireland. There aren't Irish pastures in Israel. Israel is rocky. It doesn't have expansive green pastures. It has small green patches surrounded by rocks and cliffs. In fact, the good grazing grass is often peppered with sharp rocks.

In the Christian life, that's where God makes us lie down. The green pastures are often in the middle of rocks. That's what my hospital room was: a green pasture in the middle of rocks. The Shepherd didn't invite me to lie down. He made me lie down on a very small patch of grass.

My life hasn't turned out the way I thought it would. But I have learned that is just fine. I don't have to keep running to find eternal solutions. I have learned that is an exhausting way to live. I have learned it is better to lie down regularly than to be made to lie down. How about you? Are you running hard with no rest? Are you trying hard to run out of your valley?

Maybe it's high time you stop.

Rest.

And rest in him.

CHAPTER SEVEN

Finding Calm in the Chaos

He leads me beside still waters.

—Psalm 23:2b

The Good Shepherd makes us lie down because he knows that we need rest. He knows that we need more than rest, however. He knows that we need water for our souls. And he knows that we need water that's readily available. Sheep won't drink water shooting out from fire hydrants. Neither will they drink from rapidly flowing waters. They need still waters so they can take a drink.

So here's what the Good Shepherd might say: "I will lead you to the still waters, where you can drink." Once we get there, he doesn't force us to drink; that's our role. His role is to lead us.

When was the last time you were really thirsty? I mean, when you thought you were going to die of thirst—thirsty. Depression, despair, and discouragement can feel like an unquenchable thirst. The more you look for relief, the more frustrated you become. You get really thirsty sometimes. You may have that unquenchable thirst right now. Good news! Our Shepherd actually knows where you can find water.

Sometimes the Good Shepherd leads us to fresh water in the form of a good physician. That can include a complete physical to identify any organic issues going on with you physically, and when appropriate medication could be part of the holistic solution of "fresh water."

The Good Shepherd knows the location of good, clean water. We've already seen that sheep are not the brightest creatures. If they are thirsty and they come across polluted, brackish water, they will go ahead and drink it. Then they develop parasites and disease and may even die. They need the discernment of the shepherd, and so do we.

In seasons of discouragement, it is easy to settle for polluted water. Remember the seven seductions in chapter five? They are a very real temptation when we are not allowing the Good Shepherd to meet our needs.

> In seasons of discouragement, it is easy to settle for polluted water.

God knows from which water we need to drink. Remember what Jesus said to the woman at the well in John 4? He said (paraphrasing), "You drink the water from this physical well, and you have to come back here every day to get some more. But if you drink from the water that I give you, you'll never thirst again."

Jesus knows what water we need. You may recall the time when you first came to Christ. (Some people don't, but a lot of people do.) It may have been on a campus, in a classroom, in a cubical, or around a campfire. Wherever it was, it wasn't *your* idea; God initiated your encounter with him. In the same way, the Good Shepherd leads us to the well of eternal life and ongoing spiritual renewal that is only found in him. Only he can satisfy our thirst.

He continues to do that with each of us. Sometimes we wonder if he is even near the field we're in. Not only is he near, he's leading us right now, wherever we are. You are not lost in your valley. You have to trust that the Shepherd is there and leading you. That's a wonderful thing about Jesus. He leads. He's not a backseat driver, pointing out to us where we should have turned a half-mile back. No, he *leads* us. The Shepherd is not in the driver's seat of your car; he's in the car in *front* of you. All you have to do is follow. Don't second-guess him, his Word, or his leading. This can require great faith since your feelings may not be along for the ride all the time. Share with him your fears of following, and then reach deep into God's reservoir of grace and choose to follow him despite how you feel.

I love how David expresses this in Psalm 139:3–5. He writes of the Good Shepherd:

> *You search out my path and my lying down*
> *and are acquainted with all my ways.*
> *Even before a word is on my tongue,*
> *behold, O Lord, you know it altogether.*
> *You hem me in, behind and before,*
> *and lay your hand upon me.*

God knows where he is going, which makes him a great leader to follow. He is out in front of us. He is the Alpha and the Omega. He is the beginning and the end, the first and the last. He is already there at the place you have never been but need to go.

You may say, "Yeah, but you don't understand. I have a doctor's appointment next week. The news may be bad." God's already there. "Well, wait a minute, my kids are leaving for college and the empty nest is coming. I don't know how I'm going to make it." Jesus is already there in that moment. "Yeah, but my marriage is going sideways, and we've got an appointment with a marriage counselor in two weeks, and I think it's going to be explosive." Your Shepherd is already in that room. He's hemmed you in, behind and before. Nothing catches God, the Good Shepherd, off guard.

God doesn't check Facebook for updates. He's there before the updates happen. God never has an aha moment. God has never just discovered something. God is never brought up to speed on what's happening in your life. He is keenly aware of your location in the dark valley. He already has the best route through the darkness. Sure, we may question his leading, but he has already told us in Isaiah 55:8–9 that his thoughts are not our thoughts, and his ways are not our ways. So when we say "I think," he reminds us that those are not his thoughts. When we say, "I have a way," he again reminds us that our way is not his way. "Trust me," he says.

One of the psalms that was so rich to me during my pancreatitis episode was Psalm 91. Verse 11 says, "For he will command his angels concerning you to guard you in all your ways." Isn't that cool that our Shepherd has every resource in heaven at his disposal, including angels? He's sitting in heaven while I'm on earth, overwhelmed by fear, and he simply says to the angel Gabriel and company, "Get down there and help Smith!" And just like that, they're on their way to help me.

You may be familiar with the missionary Jim Elliot. He was a gifted speaker with a promising future as a preacher. But God called him and some other men to take the gospel to an unreached people group in Ecuador. In January 1956, Jim and four fellow missionaries in their 20s flew into the territory of the Auca Indians to try to make a first contact with them. The Indians came out to them along the river and speared all five of them to death. Just like that, their ministry was over. They never had a chance to share the gospel.

They all had young wives, and some had children. In one bloody afternoon, their wives became widows, and their kids became fatherless. What possible good could come from such a tragedy? How does God's promise in Romans 8:28 that all things work together for good hold true in light of something like that?

If you study missions, you quickly realize that after 1956, they exploded around the world. The story of these men circled the globe, and Americans in particular went out by the thousands to take the gospel overseas. Millions of people came to Christ because God used the faithfulness of these men to greatly increase mission work around the world. In your personal darkness, trust his purposeful plan. Your dark valley might not be just about you. It might be far bigger than you.

Some of the wives who had been widowed went to those same Auca Indians, lived with them, and shared the gospel with them. Many in the tribe came to Christ, including the men who killed the missionaries. Some of them are still alive today. Only God can write a story like that.

You say, "Well, that's a wonderful story, but where were the angels? Where were they in that moment?"

Good question. And if you read the personal testimonies of the men who killed the missionaries and are now Christ-followers, they say that when they were spearing missionaries to death, they saw some bright beings standing next to the men and over their heads, looking heavenward.

Where were the angels? They were right there. God was not absent. He was very present.

Trust that he is leading you right now despite appearances or feelings to the contrary. Fresh water is coming to you, too. You are not an exception. The Good Shepherd hasn't forgotten about you. Here is some fresh-water thinking I ran across recently that helped quench my thirsty mind.

If you woke up this morning with more health than illness, you are more blessed than millions who will not survive this week.

If you have never experienced the danger of battle, the loneliness of imprisonment, the agony of torture, or the pangs of starvation, you are better off than 5 million people in the world.

If you can attend a church meeting, or even not attend one, without fear of harassment, arrest, torture, or death, you are more blessed than three billion people in the world.

If you have food in the refrigerator, clothes on your back, a roof overhead, and a place to sleep, you are richer than 75 percent in of the people this world.

If you have money in the bank or in your wallet or spare change in a dish someplace, you rank among the top 8 percent in the world in terms of wealth.

If you can read the Bible, you are more blessed than two billion people in the world who cannot read at all.[1]

I realize many people don't wake up in the morning with all these things, feeling blessed. Many are in the valley with extreme loss, sickness, and hunger. But it's possible to find even the smallest abundance in seasons of scarcity when we look for it, trusting God to provide for us.

Our Good Shepherd makes us lie down in green pastures so we have rest, and he leads us beside still waters to quench our thirst. In the process, he restores our tired, anxious souls. That's the wonderful reality that we'll look at in the next chapter.

He is so very close. Keep looking up.

CHAPTER EIGHT

Hit the Reset Button on Your Life

He restores my soul.

—Psalm 23:3a

In chapter seven, we highlighted two things that are true: Americans are exhausted, and Americans are depressed. We are all candidates for the care of a good shepherd.

Fortunately, we have one. As we saw, our Good Shepherd knows how to take care of sheep like us. He makes us lie down in green pastures. He leads us beside quiet waters.

He does a third vital thing as well. *He restores our souls*. This restoration in a dark valley is so essential. What exactly does that mean? In simple terms, it means he puts us back on our feet spiritually. You might feel like you've stumbled and fallen; the Good Shepherd will lift you back up.

If you study sheep, you'll learn that they have these massive wool coats, and they get very top-heavy, especially when it rains and their coats get wet or when their coats get filled with dirt. In fact, they flip over very easily. The phrase for it is become *cast*. A sheep that is cast is on its back, legs up in the air, flailing, and unable to right itself. Of course, they are easy prey for every predator until they finally get back on their feet. Often, the shepherd has to help them flip back over.

How many days have we been on our backs like this, flailing away, trying to right ourselves? In how many parenting situations have we been on our backs, asking, "How do I...?" In how many marriage moments have we needed a Shepherd who will flip us back over to right-side-up thinking? This may be you right now, flipped over and feet firmly planted in mid-air.

Many times, King David was like a sheep on its back, flailing away. He wrote, despairingly, "Why are you cast down, O my soul, and why are you in turmoil within me?" (Ps. 42:11). He was in deep despair.

A sheep is cast over. A human is cast down. You can love Jesus and still battle despair. Many men and women in the Bible were, at times, in despair. They were depressed. David. Job. Jacob. Jeremiah. Mary Magdalene. The list could go on and on.

Christians tell the most lies on Sunday. When we are at church, we try to pretend that everything is always fine. "How are you doing?" "Oh, fine. I'm fine." We're really dying on the inside, but we can't possibly let anyone know that.

Jesus, the Good Shepherd, already knows that. And he is in the business of dealing with men and women who are in the midst of despair and depression. He knows how to restore our souls. He replenishes, resets, and refills us. We need our tanks refilled. So many of us are running on fumes. Jesus is constantly in the business of refilling our tanks. So many of us are like a computer that has collected a bunch of malware. We need to be wiped clean. We need to be reset. That's what Jesus does, every single day. His mercies are new every morning (Lam. 3:23). His manna is enough for today.

How do we know when our souls need rest? How do we know when the Shepherd wants to restore our souls? I've found the following indicators to be pretty reliable.

First, everyone is bothering you. We have a saying in my house: If one person is bothering you, the issue may well be them. If two people are bothering you, the issue may well be them. When *everybody* is bothering you, it's not them—it's you. When everybody seems like an idiot, it's you. When everybody appears to be wrong, it's you. When everybody is irritating you, your soul needs some attention; it needs some restoration.

Second, you know you need soul restoration when you can't sleep consistently. Either you can't get to sleep, you can't get up from sleep, or you have trouble staying asleep. You wake up in the morning after a solid eight hours of sleep and instead of saying "Good morning, Lord," you say, "Good Lord, it's morning."

Third, you react easily and angrily. You're like a celery stick—you just snap. You're sitting at the dinner table and cute little Suzy accidentally bumps the milk. It spills on the table and drips onto the floor, and you jump all over Suzy. "Why did you do that? I told you don't ever knock the milk over!" The other people are sitting there at the table thinking, "Wow, it's just milk. We'll wipe it up." You know what you need? You need your soul restored.

Fourth, you fall consistently and easily into temptation. There's no battle to it. You just fall. You're like an army that raises the white flag when the enemy just shows up on the battlefield. There's no fight in you at all. You don't fight. You just think, "I know I'm going to sin, so what's the point?" You need to be restored.

Fifth, most conversations feel like an argument to you. Your spouse says, "Where do you want to go to dinner?" and you go into defense mode. Your teenager wants to go to the mall, and you start giving them the third degree. Hey, it's just the mall. It's just a dinner out. That's something you're supposed to enjoy, isn't it?

Sixth, your soul needs restoration when the things that used to bring you joy now seem like work. The things that used to breathe life into you—being with your kids, being with your spouse, being on vacation, going for a walk or a run—it's work; it's drudgery to you. You're not finding pleasure in the simple blessings that God brings into your life.

Finally, you lack focus or motivation. You get up in the morning, and you just can't get motivated about anything. Life seems like an endless series of tasks that you don't want to do. You have a hard time focusing. Your attention constantly wanders. You're restless.

This list isn't exhaustive, of course. But it's indicative. When several of these things are true about you, it's a sure sign that your soul needs restoration.

Now the million-dollar question is this: How do our souls get restored? After all, the verse says that God restores our souls. So how does that work? Does that mean we just say, "Lord, I see that my soul needs restoration. Would you please restore it?" and poof, it's done? Is this like a Christian car wash where I just drive through and come out the other end restored and ready to go?

No. Paul wrote to the Philippians that God began a good work in us, and he will bring it to completion (Phil. 1:6). God is working in us, both to will and to act for his good pleasure (Phil. 2:13). Paul also said in the previous verse that we are to work out our own salvation with fear and trembling (Phil. 2:12). The point is that's it's a partnership. What God works into us, we have to work out in our lives, by his grace.

So God restores us. He is working on us. And he is also working with us. So how do we partner with God to bring refreshment and restoration to our souls?

Confession and repentance

First and foremost, we partner with God through confession and repentance. After David committed adultery and murder, he knew he had sinned before the nation. He wrote in Psalm 51:

> *Wash me thoroughly from my iniquity*
> *and cleanse me from my sin!*
> *For I know my transgressions,*
> *and my sin is ever before me.*

Then he said in verse 12, "Restore to me the joy of your salvation." Thomas Brooks, a Puritan author, called repentance "the vomit of the soul." It may not be pretty, but it's got to come out. You've got to confess and repent. A Christ-follower who is mired in sin and hiding it will become completely exhausted. The most exhausting thing for your soul is hidden sin. It is absolutely depleting to the Christian. So restoration starts with confession and repentance.

Prayer

Second, get on your knees in prayer. I say *on your knees* intentionally. Don't toss up a Hail Mary prayer: "Hey Lord, I'm tired. Please restore me today." No, get on your knees, on your face, before the Lord, and say with all your heart, "Lord, I need restoration." It always convicts me when I read the Gospels and see that Jesus went off and prayed even when he was tired. That's how he got restored. He went off by himself to a quiet place and prayed. When seeking God in the dark valleys, it is best to position yourself low so he can lift you up.

This is not natural. When I'm tired, I want a bowl of cereal. I want ESPN. Jesus says something like this:

"Here's the deal. When you want restoration, what you really need is the Good Shepherd who can restore your soul. Get on your knees, on your face before the Lord, and say, 'Lord, I can't keep going here. I need you.'"

Scripture

Third, feed on the Word consistently. Just as you physically need food for energy, your soul needs spiritual food. It needs the Word of God. Check out Psalm 119. It is 176 verses on what the Word of God does in your life. Don't fall into the trap of thinking you don't have enough time to read God's Word. You don't have the time to *not* be in the Word. I often say to our church family, "Get off Facebook and get your face in his book."

In the dark valleys of life, we have to obey the way we want to feel. That sounds odd, I know. Obey the way you *want* to feel. Don't obey the way you actually *do* feel. No change happens—no good change at least—when we obey what we feel all the time. "I don't feel like reading the Word. I don't feel like praying. I don't feel like forgiving this person." God's commands aren't spoken to your feelings. Neither are his promises. We say to God, "Lord, I don't feel like reading your Word, but I'm going to obey because I want to feel restored." So we do, and we get the results we want. We are blessed. We are restored. Quick? No. Easy? No. But this is how you must fight in the valley— by faith.

Sleep and diet

Fourth, take a look at your sleep regimen and your diet. *Seriously?* you might be thinking. "That doesn't sound that spiritual." If that's what we think, we've bought into a false understanding of how God has created us. We have a body and a soul, and they are unified into one person. We are not to think of our souls as important and our bodies as irrelevant. That was the thinking of the Greek Gnostics during the time of the early church. "Only the spirit counts," they said. "It doesn't matter what we do with our bodies." They were simply justifying their bodily sins, but unfortunately that dualistic thinking crept into the church. The truth is that God has made us one person, body and soul, seamlessly united together. What happens to our souls affects our bodies, and what happens to our bodies affects our souls. If our souls need to be restored, it may be that we need to get more sleep and start eating fruits and vegetables instead of ice cream and chips. God has given us amazing bodies, and sometimes we simply need to take care of them. It means that if you're exhausted, you might do well to see your doctor for a complete physical.

Exercise

Fifth, spend regular time moving your body, playing, taking healthy diversions, enjoying and appreciating creation. Let me show you how this works. How does an atheist realize that God exists? One way is through general revelation, God's creation. In Romans 1:20, Paul said, "*For his invisible attributes, namely, his eternal power and divine nature, have been clearly perceived, ever since the creation of the world, in the things that have been made.*" Go stand on the valley floor of Yosemite National Park. At places and moments like that, it's hard to say that my valleys are too big for God. When you lose track of time out in creation, with exercise, or with a hobby, you are being refreshed.

Even as a Christ-follower, we can become practical atheists. What does that look like? It looks like saying in our hearts, "I love Jesus, but I'm not sure God exists in my valley right now." When you find yourself acting and believing like a practical atheist, your soul is in serious need of restoration. Getting out in creation can really help. Then we say, "Wow, look at the Milky Way. Wow, look at those majestic mountains. Wow, look at that huge ocean." Suddenly we have a new perspective, and God looks very big and our challenges look relatively small. That's the way it should be. God restores our souls. Here is a key thought: *big God, small valleys; small God, big valleys.*

> **Big God, small valleys; small God, big valleys.**

Life-giving people

Sixth, immerse yourself with godly, life-giving people. There are people in your life that I call straws. They are constantly sucking the life out of you. Take a break from them for a while. Get with people who breathe life into you. Get with God's people. We are to build each other up. We are a source of God's restoration to one another. Valleys require periods where you allow people to pour into your life.

Don't overschedule yourself

Seventh, get hold of your schedule. For many of us, the reason our souls get tired is because our schedules are out of control. You may say, "I don't have any time to do anything else." All right, I'm going to give you two and a half extra hours per week, as a free gift, and it's not even Christmas. Studies have shown that if you simply check social media six times a day, you end up spending two and a half hours a week on social media. So there you are—a free gift of more time. Just stop checking social media so often, and you'll immediately be a little less busy.

As a Christ-follower, we have to learn to say no to some things, even morally neutral things. Maybe for you it's not Facebook. It could be any of hundreds of things that are stealing your time and preventing you from experiencing God's best. I find that it's a good practice to say no to something every day. Sometime during the day, look at your spouse or a close coworker or friend and say No. Just get a no out. It doesn't mean anything; it's just for the practice. Saying no is cooperating with the Good Shepherd, who wants to give rest to your soul.

These ways that we can cooperate with God are not a formula, of course. Nothing in the Christian life is a formula. We're talking about our souls here, not math. And we're talking about a relationship with a living Savior. Every relationship is unique.

One of the most comforting and encouraging passages in the Bible is Matthew 11:28–30. "Come to me, all who labor and are heavy laden, and I will give you rest. Take my yoke upon you and learn from me, for I am gentle and lowly in heart, and you will find rest for your souls. For my yoke is easy and my burden is light." The Christian life is not meant to be exhausting; it's meant to be challenging but relieving at the same time.

Jesus is inviting us to experience his rest right now. We can experience his rest at any time, at any place. We enter in by faith, by trusting in what he has told us. As the writer to the Hebrews said, "We who have believed enter that rest" (Heb. 4:3).

Some people find it helpful to go to a place in their minds where they feel rejuvenated. It could be a particular beach, a cove on that beach, a forest, or the mountains. Maybe there's a mountain rock you remember sitting on, overlooking endless valleys from way up high. The goal is to calm yourself by using your God-given imagination to recall a beautiful, serene experience. When Psalm 23 mentions green pastures and still waters, we use our imaginations to experience the rest and refreshment those settings provide.

Maybe you're like Jesus at the well. He sat down because he was tired. He was exhausted. Imagine yourself sitting on that rock right now, ready to be rejuvenated. The only thing you hear is the rustle of the leaves or the waves crashing. There's nobody else calling your name. Only God. And he might be saying something like this to you, his much-loved child:

> *You are chosen. You are so greatly and perfectly loved. You're alive in me. Your home is not in this world. Your home is in heaven. I am preparing a place for you right now. You are holy. Much greater is he who is in you than the enemy who is in the world. You are my workmanship. You are perfect and compete in me despite your shortcomings. You can find peace in me at all times, even now.*

There is nothing you could do right now to cause God to love you any more than he does at this very moment. You are a joint heir with Christ; you are more than a conqueror; there is nothing that will separate you from the love of Christ Jesus. In the valley he invites you in this moment to trust him, to rest in him. Just breathe and relax. When you do, he promises in Isaiah 40:31 that you will find restoration:

> But they who wait for the LORD shall renew their strength;
> they shall mount up with wings like eagles;
> they shall run and not be weary;
> they shall walk and not faint.

He has promised to deliver you from fear. He has promised that all of your needs will be supplied. He has promised to give you wisdom if you'll just ask. He has promised to come again. He has promised to end death, sorrow, and pain. He's assured you that one day you'll receive a new body.

You are greatly loved by the Good Shepherd.

He will restore your soul.

CHAPTER NINE

Getting on the Right Path

He leads me in paths of righteousness
for his name's sake.

—Psalm 23:3b

Life presents us with some deep valleys. Depression is one of them. We would never choose depression, but sometimes it chooses us.

As with all difficult seasons, especially ones that seem to go on forever, it's easy to ask the wrong question about depression. That question is *Why?* Why, God? Why do I have to go through this depression?

Why is a natural question, but it doesn't take us very far because the truth is that we often don't have a good answer for it. In eternity, we will. Right now, though, we can't see fully as God sees. We see merely shadows, not the full reality of things. One day we will be face to face with Jesus, and we will see the full reality, not the shadows.

There is a question, however, that does get us someplace, and that question is *How?* Lord, how do I walk through this valley? The peaks of life can sometimes be awesome, but the valleys can be very deep and very dark. Depression or seasons of melancholy are such valleys. We need to know how to walk through the darkness. Spurgeon wrote, "Any simpleton can follow the narrow path in the light: faith's rare wisdom enables us to march on in the dark with infallible accuracy, since she places her hand in that of her Great Guide."

> "Any simpleton can follow the narrow path in the light: faith's rare wisdom enables us to march on in the dark with infallible accuracy, since she places her hand in that of her Great Guide."

Our great guide, the Good Shepherd, often moves at a much different pace than we're expecting. We have to learn patience when we are on his path and he is our guide. Very few things in life turn out well when rushed. That includes the care of our souls. Most of the Christian life is spent in the crockpot, not the microwave. Everyone knows the tenderness of crockpot cooking. It is worth the wait. Frederick Faber, an English theologian, addresses our impatience:

> In the spiritual life God chooses to try our patience first of all by his slowness. He is slow. We are swift and precipitate. It is because we are but for a time and he has been from eternity. Thus, grace for the most part acts slowly. He works by little and by little with slowness which tries our faith because it is so great a mystery.[1]

The path God takes us on is rarely the shortest route— at least in our way of thinking. Consider the Israelites. They wandered around in the wilderness for 40 years before finally entering the promised land. They learned to trust God during that time just as we learn to trust God in times of waiting.

Mere platitudes won't help us walk through the valley of depression. We can't just recite two verses and expect this valley to disappear overnight. We need to hold on to truths from God's Word and not let go.

In Psalm 23, David told us that the Lord is our Shepherd; he cares for all our needs. We don't have any need that he doesn't provide. He provides rest, nourishment, and refreshment. David said:

> He leads me in paths of righteousness for his name's sake.
>
> —Psalm 23:3b

What does God say to us here that makes a difference when we are in the dark valley? Psalm 119:105 tells us that God's Word is a light to our path. If we don't have God's truth to light our way, the valley can get very dark indeed. What is the light that God provides for us? Here God gives us the principle of the path.

Path principle: Every path has a purpose.

David's words in Psalm 23 tell us several things. First, we are all on a path. Everybody's on a path in life. That path is about something, and it's leading us somewhere. Second, for those of us who are Christ-followers, we are being *led*. Our Shepherd leads us. As the apostle Paul declared many centuries later in Romans 8:14, "For all who are led by the Spirit of God are sons of God." Third, the path we are on is not an ordinary one. It's a path of righteousness. It's God's path. Fourth, and critically, the path we are on has a purpose. It is for God's glory. That's what "for his name's sake" means. It's for his glory. Keeping that in mind can lift our thoughts beyond our own concerns and questions.

Why is this important? Because it frames the way we think about what we're going through. And how we think about what we're going through is vital. It makes the difference between cooperating with God or resisting him through it. We want to think about things as God thinks about them, because his perspective is right.

We have mentioned this before, but if our Good Shepherd is the one leading us, he is out in front of us. You can't lead sheep from behind. They'll start going every which way. No, you have to lead from the front.

So what does that mean? Wherever we are going, Jesus is already there. He knows exactly where we are heading; he is there before us. If our lives seem

> **You have to trust that there is purpose in the path.**

to be going through a ravine, remember that he was there at the beginning of the ravine, he is with us in the middle of the ravine, and he will be there at the end of the ravine when we walk out. As someone in my church testified, "He carried us. We were right there, hanging by a thread, didn't know how we were going to do this, but he led us through that valley." You have to trust that there is purpose in the path.

You know you're heading into a valley when you say, "I don't think I can handle this." Valleys are places where we feel like we can't handle things. And our feelings are right; we *can't* handle them.

There is a myth in the church today that comes from the saying, "God doesn't give you more than you can handle."

> **While you want out, he wants in to help you walk through it.**

Well, that sounds nice, but it is neither true nor biblical. The truth is that God often gives you more than you can handle. His promise is that he will never give you more than *he* can handle (John 15:5). So you can stop trying to carry your pain in your own strength and give it to him. Often, that's the whole point of the valley. God wants to teach us that he is sufficient for us and that although we can't handle the situation, he can. He wants to teach us to depend on him. While you want out, he wants in to help you walk through it.

Is it possible that God's path of righteousness would actually be through a valley in life? Yes! He absolutely leads us into valleys so he might accomplish his great, eternal purposes in our lives and so he can use our lives for the good of others. Remember, the Spirit of God led Jesus into the desert to be tempted and tested (Matthew 4:1–11).

The word *path* literally means a way or a direction. In other words, it's Jesus calling us in a particular direction. As sheep, we are going to require a lot of care. We have to be led in everything. We have to be led to lie down. We have to be led to food. We have to be led to shelter. We have to be led to water. And like all sheep, we have a tendency to keep going astray. The goal is not just to get us out of trouble but to get us back on the path through the valley. Why? Because the path of the Shepherd produces righteousness. The valley of the shadow of death is not designed to produce happiness, at least not immediate happiness. God is not primarily concerned with our short-term happiness; he knows that left to ourselves, we tend to pursue happiness in foolish ways. So he has given us the Holy Spirit to produce holiness in our lives, not short-lived happiness.

> So he has given us the Holy Spirit to produce holiness in our lives, not short-lived happiness.

What is the path of righteousness on which God is leading us? It is simply a path defined by God's view of what is right. In other words, it reflects his character—who he is. Self-righteousness, on the other hand, consists of the things we think will make us right or at least feel right. But that's not where the Good Shepherd leads us. The righteousness by which he leads us is his righteousness, which is true righteousness.

We must trust that his path is right. Our melancholy does not necessarily mean we are on the wrong path. God has purpose in our pain. His paths are not wrong; they are always right. They are righteous paths that lead to true and lasting joy. Yes, a path of despair and discouragement has crossed the desk of God, and he has approved it for wise and loving reasons. Therefore, there is purpose in your path, no matter how painful it is at times.

Often, we wouldn't lead ourselves down the path he chooses for us. That's because we are sheep, and sheep don't know what's best for them. As Proverbs 16:25 says, "There is a way that seems right to a man, but its end is the way to death." We would choose the path of comfort. We would choose the path of ease. Sometimes, we would choose the path of unrighteousness.

> **There is a way that seems right to a man, but its end is the way to death.**

But God knows better. He knows what he wants to accomplish in our lives and what is best for us, both now and for eternity. He leads us down that path. If we are honest with ourselves, that's the path we would also want if we knew what God knows. As Christ-followers, deep down we want to be led along a path of righteousness. Instead of asking the Good Shepherd why, ask him what he wants you to learn along the path you're traveling.

So how does he lead us? How do I know I am following him in the valley? The Shepherd primarily does it in four ways—what I like to call the four s's.

By his Scripture

First, he leads us by *Scripture.* Do you want to know what God's will is? Read God's Word. God's will is God's Word.

If you want God to speak to you out loud, then read the Scriptures out loud. As we noted before in Psalm 119:105:

"Your word is a lamp to my feet and a light to my path."

If you're in a dark place, what do you do? You rush to get a flashlight. When you're in a dark valley, you need the lamp of God's Word to guide your thinking. Don't let depression keep you from the light of God's Word. Depression will whisper to you that nothing you do will help, but that is a lie. God's Word can penetrate the dark places and give you new hope.

By his Spirit

Second, the Good Shepherd leads us by his *Spirit*. The New Testament is full of this truth. Just read chapters 14–16 in John's Gospel and look for all the references to the Spirit's leading. They're everywhere. Sometimes we are aware of his leading; sometimes we aren't. In either case, the Spirit is leading us.

Our Shepherd is not just with us; he is in us through his Spirit. This reality alone is reason for great hope. The apostle Paul said of the Spirit, "Christ in you, the hope of glory" (Colossians 1:27). The Christian life is lived with Christ through the Spirit to the glory of God. We are not on our own.

The Spirit of God inside us is constantly renewing us and guiding us according to the truth of God's Word. He is present and active in times of darkness. He enables us to take every despairing thought and make it obedient to Christ (2 Corinthians 10:5).

By his servants

Third, he leads us through his *servants*. What do I mean by that? Proverbs 12:15 says, "The way of a fool is right in his own eyes, but a wise man listens to advice." God is gracious to put wise godly men and women around us to speak truth into our lives. If you're in a valley, don't be in it alone. Get with God's people. Get with life-giving, truth-speaking people of God because being alone in the valley just makes the darkness worse. Light comes from the Word of God and from the people of God, men and women who will speak life into your soul.

In our individualistic culture, we tend to shy away from reaching out to others, but we must not let our fears of rejection, weakness, or embarrassment prevent us from leaning on others during the dark times. The body of Christ is meant to support each other. We're meant to bear one another's burdens. Allowing others to help is good for you, for them, for the church, and for the kingdom.

By his sovereignty

Fourth, he leads us through his *sovereignty*. I love Proverbs 16:9, one of my favorite verses in all of Scripture: "The heart of man plans his way, but the Lord establishes his steps." Some people like to emphasize people's free will. It's in this verse. Some like to emphasize God's sovereignty. It's in this verse as well. In the Scripture, there's a dynamic tension between the two that

> The heart of man plans his way, but the Lord establishes his steps.

we can spend our whole lives trying to figure out, or that we can simply accept as reality. The path of faith is to accept both as reality.

What Proverbs 16:9 tells us is that God has sovereign control of your life. What, practically, does that mean? It means he always has the last word. He has the last word about where he leads you. He has the last word about leading you into a ravine, and he has the last word about leading you out of a valley.

But you might say, "I got into this valley because _____" (you fill in the blank). My company laid me off. My investments went south. My spouse left me. My child rebelled. My parents neglected me.

Okay, any of those things may be true. But God has the last word. He is in sovereign control over the circumstances of your life.

"But I got myself into this ravine," you say. "Look at my mistakes. I made this bed for myself, and now I have to lie in it and be miserable." God can't steer a parked car, so you have to take the first step. And when you do, he opens up a path.

True, your mistakes or even your biology may have contributed to your being where you are today. Who among us can't say that? But God has the last word. His sovereignty extends even to your own bad choices. He led you to where you are, and he will lead you where you need to go. In the meantime, he will shape your character and accomplish good in your life in ways you could never have imagined.

We've already mentioned that God led his own Son into a dark valley. It's worth repeating and remembering that after Jesus was baptized by John the Baptist, he was led by the Spirit into the wilderness to be tempted by the devil for 40 days and 40 nights while fasting (Matthew 4:1–2). This was not a meaningless detour from God's path; it was a necessary time of preparation for what was ahead.

Consider what this experience must have been like for Jesus—no food, exhausted, among wild beasts, and tempted by Satan. Not exactly a refreshing spiritual retreat before embarking on his ministry.

But also consider what happened after Jesus walked through that valley with the Father. In Luke 4:14, we are told that "Jesus returned in the power of the Spirit to Galilee." The valley Jesus went through was not without purpose; it was to strengthen his trust in the Father and empower him for ministry.

What else does the Bible have to say about the temptations of Christ? Listen to Hebrews 2:18 and 4:15:

> *For because he himself has suffered when tempted, he is able to help those who are being tempted. For we do not have a high priest who is unable to sympathize with our weaknesses, but one who in every respect has been tempted as we are, yet without sin.*

Jesus's valley was not without purpose, and neither is yours. God's sovereignty is still operating, even in those moments when he allows us to walk through deep, dark valleys of depression. There is no growth without pruning. There are no diamonds without pressure. There is no gold without fire. God's goal in our suffering is that we would share in his holiness. He is out to conform us to the very image of his Son, Jesus Christ (Romans 8:29).

God will do whatever is necessary to change us into his Son's likeness. Why? Because that is what he created us for, and that is what he, in his love, knows is best for us. Since we are his children, he isn't going to let us run off and abandon the right path. What loving Father would allow his children to do that? So he refines us through difficulty and darkness. He allows us to walk through the dark valley, knowing that we will emerge changed and better than before. His goal for us is not a depression-free existence, but rather freedom from sin. In our weakness, he is strength.

While we're in the valley, we don't like it. It doesn't feel good. Nobody likes to be in the fire. Nobody likes the pressure. Nobody likes the deep, dark ravines. But fortunately, God doesn't do things according to our temporary wants; he does what's best for us.

The last phrase of Psalm 23:3 sheds additional light on what God is up to in allowing our dark valley experiences. It says, *"He leads me in paths of righteousness for his name's sake"* (emphasis added). Your season of depression actually has more to do with him than with you. You are telling a story about him through your life and through your response to suffering, including depression. The phrase "his name's sake" simply means that it is for the glory of God.

We all have glory. Your personal name is your glory. Your glory is the first thing that comes to people's minds when they hear your name. Hear someone say Abraham Lincoln, and immediately you retrieve from your mind

> **The goal of the Christian life is not to get undepressed but to give glory to God.**

your conception of what kind of person Abraham Lincoln was. Hear someone say Adolph Hitler, and an entirely different idea comes to mind. Their names are their glory, so to speak. God leads us in paths of righteousness so he may be glorified. When people see what God has done in your life, he receives the glory due his name.

God's glory in your walking through the valley is tied to his love. "God is love," the Bible tells us (1 John 4:8). Love isn't simply something God does; it's who he is. And love is entirely other-focused. Love always does what is best for the other person. Love always lays its life down for the other. Love is always self-giving, not self-getting.

So when God glorifies himself, it is an act of love because he only does what is best for his creation, including his people. If you think about it, it makes sense. All creation is meant to live in perfect harmony with God. It only lives in perfect harmony when it glorifies, exalts, and manifests the one who made it—because he is perfectly good and worthy of all glory and honor and praise.

Creation's highest good is glorifying its Creator. Anything other than that is a perversion of purpose and destructive. And we see that in the world all around us. Humanity doesn't seek to glorify God first, and the result is a complete mess of sin and suffering.

Jesus came to restore us to God and to our highest good. Our highest good is that God is glorified. He knows that, and he will not settle for anything less in our lives than our highest good. That's why he leads us in paths of righteousness. Our suffering is not an indication that God doesn't love us. God supremely deserves to be glorified, yes, but he also seeks his own glory *because of his infinite love for us.*

It's like a good father demanding respect from his children. He does it not because he can't make it without their respect. He does it because he knows that disrespecting him is destructive for them.

So God is intent on this purpose: that our lives glorify him. And he leads us in paths of righteousness to accomplish that purpose. And sometimes those paths take us into dark places. And in that, even that, we can rejoice, knowing that God is lovingly accomplishing what is best for us. That's why James can tell us to *"Count it all joy, my brothers, when you meet trials of various kinds"* (James 1:2), and why Peter says, *"In this you rejoice, though now for a little while, if necessary, you have been grieved by various trials"* (1 Pet. 1:6).

It doesn't feel good while we are in it. God *knows* it doesn't feel good. God takes no pleasure in your pain. That's why Peter acknowledges that his readers were distressed. Feeling distressed is not something we want for ourselves. Nobody loves the pain and the pressure, but God is doing something important in our lives. God picks glory over comfort every time. Just ask John the Baptist. He died a martyr's death. Just ask Lazarus. His good friend, Jesus, let him die. Just ask Mary and Martha, who suffered their brother's death. *Just ask Jesus, who went to the cross.* And look at the perfect goodness of God that came from all of it.

> **God takes no pleasure in your pain.**

The Good Shepherd loves us perfectly. He has us on a path. He leads us. He leads us down paths of righteousness. Sometimes those paths take us into difficult valleys. But he has not abandoned us. It's just the opposite. He is working everything for our good. He is restoring us to everything we were designed to be. And he will complete the good work that he has begun in us.

You are safe in his sovereignty.

Keep walking.

PROMISES OF THE SHEPHERD

I note that some whom I greatly love and esteem, who are, in my judgment, among the very choicest of God's people, nevertheless travel most of the way to heaven by night.

—Charles Spurgeon

CHAPTER TEN

Essential Perspectives in the Valley

Even though I walk through the valley of the shadow of death…

—Psalm 23:4a

I'm not much of a hiker, unless it's to the refrigerator. But in California, where I live, there are lots of canyons to hike. And I've put on the boots (or at least my sneakers) and tried my feet at hiking into them (and, I hoped, back out of them) a few times.

I've learned this about walking in a canyon. When you're down there, it's hard to get perspective, especially when you haven't hiked that path before. You're not sure where the next bend will take you, how much farther down you have to go before you mercifully start to go up, or how much longer the hike will actually last. You're on a path, but there are plenty of unknowns.

Life is like that. Walking through a valley is like that. Walking through a dark time is like that.

The thing we have to accept is that life is full of valleys. Life is full of low points. It's never a matter of *if* we will be in a valley; it's a matter of *when*. There are only two types of Christians: those coming out of a trial and those heading into a trial. And when we are in one, we have to accept that it is the valley we are meant to walk through. God is sovereign. We aren't there by accident. But we won't die in the valley. We *will* get through it. The difficult thing is that we must learn to walk through it. We can't sprint through it. There's no shortcut because God intends to do some things in our lives and through our lives while we're there. So we must learn to walk with him through it.

When we are in a dark valley, faced with unknowns, what we really need is perspective. If only we could magically rise above the valley and get a bird's-eye view, we would realize where we are heading and how we can get there. And we would know that we will eventually come out on the other side.

But when we are in life's valleys, we can't magically rise out of them. That is, we usually can't extricate ourselves from the valley. If we could, we

> The way out of the valley of despair, discouragement, and depression is the way through the valley.

would! We have no choice but to go through, sight unseen.

But there's another way to get a bird's-eye view. It's the way of faith, and it's God's way. Because God calls us in 2 Corinthians 4:18 to *"look not to the things that are seen but to the things that are unseen. For the things that are seen are transient, but the things that are unseen are eternal."*

So when we are in the valley, how do we let God lead us through? How do we see as he sees? How can we consistently look at what is unseen, not at what is seen? I have found the following to be both biblical and tried and true in the lives of many Christ-followers. Each begins with the letter *P* to remind you they are a *priority* in the valley.

1. Posture

How does God lead us through the valley of darkness? Depression can seem so pointless. That's one of the worst things about it. We've got to learn to take God's perspective on all things, and that can mean not trusting how we feel. Remember, feelings feel; the only thing feelings can do is feel. They do not reason. You must choose to reason. We have to get control of our thoughts. Remember, much of the Christian life happens between the ears. Usually, the most important thing to grab hold of is this: God's got you covered. You really can trust him!

"I don't feel very covered," you say. Even so, God's got you covered. "But I don't feel very covered," you repeat.

The question is: What are you going to believe? Are you going to believe what you feel or what God says? Let me urge you to adopt God's perspective. Choose to see things as God sees them. Why? Because the God of the Bible has proved himself faithful in every way throughout history and in the lives of all his people.

Consider that our God is omnipresent. That is, he's everywhere, including always where we are. We have not been abandoned. In Psalm 139:7–10, David wrote:

> *Where shall I go from your Spirit?*
> *Or where shall I flee from your presence?*
> *If I ascend to heaven, you are there!*
> *If I make my bed in Sheol, you are there!*
> *If I take the wings of the morning*
> *and dwell in the uttermost parts of the sea,*
> *even there your hand shall lead me,*
> *and your right hand shall hold me.*

Not only is God omnipresent, he's also sovereign. That means he's in control of everything, including what is happening in your life. He isn't on his throne sipping on Maalox saying, "Michael, I can't figure out this one. This is stressing me out. I don't know how to help so and so." David continued in Psalm 139:11–12:

> *If I say, "Surely the darkness shall cover me,*
> *and the light about me be night,"*
> *even the darkness is not dark to you;*
> *the night is bright as the day,*
> *for darkness is as light with you.*

David wrote in Psalm 103:19, "*The Lord has established his throne in the heavens, and his kingdom rules over all.*" God is sovereign. Nothing catches him flat-footed. Does that make our struggles easy? No, but it does bring comfort and encouragement and faith that he is working things out in our lives according to his plan. It does give us hope in the dark valley of depression and despair.

2. Plan

You need a plan to get through your depression or any painful trial. What do I mean by this? Any godly man or woman who would come alongside you is going to tell you that after you go through a deep loss or a deep trial, you will have to find a new normal. You say, "Well, it's not like it used to be." You're right, it's not. There's been loss. "My kid's not at home anymore," you say. I understand. Life is going to be different now. It's not the same. You may have lost a job you loved, or your marriage may have fallen apart. When these kinds of things happen, there's a new normal coming eventually, and it won't be so painful. When is it going to come? I don't know. You're on God's timeline, and things don't often happen immediately there. It could take a while.

In the meantime, you have to find a plan to help you keep putting one foot in front of the other. This could literally mean going for a walk every day to clear out your head a little and move your body. It could mean reaching out to friends for regular, scheduled time together. It could mean some professional counseling. It will no doubt mean committing to spending time in the Scriptures and in prayer, no matter how you feel.

Occupy yourself with a big project or many projects that direct your mind off of yourself and onto others. There is no end to the number of nursing home residents, hospitalized patients, struggling families, volunteer organizations, and ministries that need a helping hand. Do not sit around and wait for your problems to disappear. Busy yourself with projects and invest your time in caring for others.

3. Perseverance

Trials are the places where God teaches us perseverance. This is a brutal beauty of this life. And depression is often a trial of the severest kind. James writes in James 1:2–4:

> *Count it all joy, my brothers, when you meet trials of various kinds, for you know that the testing of your faith produces steadfastness. And let steadfastness have its full effect, that you may be perfect and complete, lacking in nothing.*

Do we want to be people who are able to endure, to have steadfastness? Trials are the arenas in which we learn how to do that. Trials teach us that we must depend on God for what we need. The illusion of self-sufficiency gets demolished through trials. This is a "severe mercy" because apart from pain, we would go on trying to live by our own strength, which is woefully inadequate to the demands life places on us.

So we pray for two things: *endurance*, or the ability to stay in the valley while God has us there, and, as James said in verses 5 and 6, *wisdom*, the ability to learn what God wants us to learn while we're in the valley.

Of course, in the middle of a trial, it's very hard to see the benefits of what we're going through. Honestly, we're usually much more interested in experiencing some relief than in learning lessons or becoming deeper, more empathetic, loving people. But God's love for us is a refining love. He thinks long term; we think short term. He thinks holiness and lasting joy; we think comfort and immediate happiness. Thankfully, he is too wise and too kind to not provide for us what we really need—to be conformed to the image of his Son.

Joy is a key word that James uses. Happiness is a cultural construct that really disappoints. Happy works for Happy Meals but not in a dark valley. Even the etymology of the word *happy* expresses the randomness of feeling happy. Our word *happy* comes from the root word *hap*, which means random, chance, or accident. From the root, we get words like haphazard, happenstance, and happy. You get the point. If you and I experience happiness, it is random chance. That is why you can fake happy, but you can't fake joy. Joy is a discipline. The best definition of joy was given to me by a friend, Paul Sailhamer: "Joy is the deep down settled confidence that God is in control of every detail of your life." Joy is connected to your mind, not your feelings.

4. Promise

You're in a deep, dark valley—a deep, dark place. You feel down and out. Your depression doesn't seem to be lifting anytime soon. You desperately need a promise from God Almighty. "Lord, what's your will?" Remember, God's will is God's Word. There is no substitute for getting into his Word. I love how 2 Peter 1:3–4 talks about the power of God's promises to help us become overcomers:

> *His divine power has granted to us all things that pertain to life and godliness, through the knowledge of him who called us to his own glory and excellence, by which he has granted to us*

his precious and very great promises, so that through them you may become partakers of the divine nature.

You need to find a promise that you can grip onto, and I mean a single promise that becomes your lifeline through that valley. In some of the valleys I've been through, I've held onto Isaiah 43:2:

When you pass through the waters, I will be with you; and through the rivers, they shall not overwhelm you; when you walk through fire you shall not be burned, and the flame shall not consume you.

Those verses have been to me like an oxygen tank to a fireman on the third floor of a burning building. They breathe life into me. In those deep, dark moments when my head hits the pillow along with my tears, I stand on the promises of God and say, "Lord, you are sovereign. I will not be burned by this."

5. Praise

This is a big one and often overlooked. So few do it well. When we are in a dark valley, when we are going through depression, we seem to have the gifts of complaining and criticism. It just doesn't seem reasonable to praise the Lord when everything looks bleak. If anything, we tend to be angry at God for allowing whatever predicament we find ourselves in, so we feel justified in complaining without hope. You're not unusual to feel that way. That's a very natural reaction to suffering. And the Psalms clearly show that God wants us to be honest with him. That being said, we must do more than complain and adopt a negative, hopeless attitude. We must choose to respond with faith and offer a sacrifice of praise.

As the above verses from 2 Peter highlight, Christians live a supernatural life. The God of all the universe has come to live within us. His divine nature is within us. And what does he say to do when everything looks bleak? He says to praise him. What's supernatural is to praise him, because praise reveals where we are choosing to place our trust—not in the circumstances our eyes can see, but in the unseen One who is causing all things to work together for our good, even when it doesn't seem like it.

Look at Job's response to his trials. He lost everything: family, wealth, health. You name it, he lost it. This was his response:

> *Naked I came from my mother's womb, and naked shall I return. The Lord gave, and the Lord has taken away; blessed be the name of the Lord.*
>
> —Job 1:21

Do you think Job felt like offering praise to God? He had just lost everything. His children were dead. His business was destroyed. Yet he praised God anyway. He chose to believe that, despite his feelings and circumstances, God was worthy to be praised, he was worthy to be trusted. Job trusted that God knew what he was doing; he trusted that God's love would not fail.

God's goodness, his power, and his love still do not fail. We are not an exception to God's goodness, even if we are currently feeling depressed. So we can and must choose to praise him, even when everything looks dark— especially when everything looks dark.

I stumbled across a prayer of thanksgiving in a 1999 issue of *Family Circle* magazine. It elicits praise and thankfulness because of the perspective it sees in life. Take a moment to let the words of this prayer soak into your heart:

I am thankful for:

> ...the mess to clean after a party because it means I have been surrounded by friends.

> ...the taxes I pay because it means that I am employed.

> ...the clothes that fit a little too snug because it means I have enough to eat.

> ...my shadow who watches me work because it means I am out in the sunshine.

> ...a lawn that needs mowing, windows that need cleaning and gutters that need fixing because it means that I have a home.

> ...the spot I find at the far end of the parking lot because it means I am capable of walking.

> ...all the complaining I hear about our government because it means we have freedom of speech.

> ...my huge heating bill because it means that I am warm.

> ...the lady behind me in church who sings off key because it means I can hear.

> ...the piles of laundry and ironing because it means my loved ones are nearby.

...the alarm that goes off in the early morning hours because it means that I'm alive.

...weariness and aching muscles at the end of the day because it means I have been productive.[1]

6. People

You're in a dark valley, and here more than ever it is true: it is not good for humans to be alone. When life gets really difficult, our natural response is to isolate ourselves. *I can't deal with people right now*, we think. *I have to get alone.* Remember, behave the way you *want* to feel.

Again, that's a very natural reaction to pain. Many times, there is some shame attached to loss or trials—we want to seem like we've got it all together all the time—so we try to get better on our own. This can be especially true when our losses cause us to sink into depression. Sadly, there can still be a stigma attached to depression, despite the fact that many, many people go through low times.

We need, by the Spirit of God, to pursue what's supernatural. And what's supernatural is to put ourselves with other believers who will speak the word of life, the word of truth to us, so that when we begin to question the very character of God, they can gently but firmly steer us back to the truth.

David wrote, *"Even though I walk through the valley of the shadow of death, I will fear no evil, for you are with me"* (Ps. 23:4). I love the honesty. He doesn't say there is no evil; there obviously is. Here's a news flash: following Jesus has dark valleys, and there's a lot of evil around us. But we can choose not to fear the evil. Why? Because we're going to stick our heads in the sand? No. Because we're not alone.

Notice that David says, "You are with me." Our Savior's name is Immanuel, meaning "God with us." Nobody in this room can say, "I'm completely alone." You have a Shepherd who's leading you.

So many times, I hear people say, "If I had lived back when Jesus lived and had seen all those miracles, I could've walked through these deep, dark valleys." But they have it wrong. Don't wish you could go back to the time of Jesus. Jesus said in John 16:7 that it's better for him to leave so the Spirit may come. We have the Spirit of God in us. Paul says in Colossians 1:27 that Christ in us is the hope of glory.

If you are walking next to someone who is going through a dark valley, remember this: It's better for you to be *with* them than to be *wordy*. People need our presence, not our preaching. It's okay to say, "I just don't know what to say." Don't say anything. Just be with them and walk through that valley with them, because that's what Jesus is doing, too.

7. Perspective

To walk through the valley, we have to get a bird's-eye, or a God's-eye, view. The ultimate God's-eye view is to see things in light of eternity.

Centuries ago, back when I was in school, we used to construct timelines. We would take a piece of paper and a pencil and draw a timeline that looked a bit like a ruler. Then we would put points on the timeline where things had happened in our lives.

Imagine that you have a measuring tape—one of the old, flexible ones that you stretch out by hand, not the ones that retract automatically. The tape is yellow, remember? But the first part of the tape you've colored blue. The blue part stretches from your living room to the front door.

At the front door, the tape is yellow again. And it keeps going. It goes past the next house or apartment and the next one and the next one. It goes all the way down the street. It goes all the way through your town and to the next town and the next town and into the countryside and across the country. It crosses the ocean and circles the earth, and then it starts wrapping around the earth—five times, ten times, a hundred times, a million times. You finally lose track of the number of times, and yet it still keeps going.

This tape is your life. The blue part, inside your house, is this time right now on earth. It has a beginning, lasts a little while, and pretty quickly reaches the door. Then the fun part starts, because out the door, we enter into eternity. Life never ends, and it's full of boundless joy and adventure and love and peace—fulfillment beyond imagination.

The blue part, inside the house, has to navigate around some furniture. It gets frayed. It gets stains on it. Its color dulls over the years. It sometimes goes all the way down to the floor and gets stepped on.

And the blue part is really, really short. Often, we are afflicted in the blue part. But the afflictions are light and momentary. Do they seem light and momentary? No, they seem heavy and like they'll last forever.

But in the grand scheme of things, they aren't, and they won't. They are light and momentary. God says so. And you know what? This momentary, light affliction is producing for us an eternal weight of glory far beyond all comparison (2 Corinthians 4:17). That's good news. That produces real, lasting, unshakable hope. Peter wrote:

> *And after you have suffered a little while, the God of all grace, who called you to his eternal glory in Christ, will himself restore, confirm, strengthen, and establish you.*
>
> —1 Peter 5:10

That is seeing as God sees. And holding onto that reality is walking through the valley, one step at a time, with the Good Shepherd.

You are saved.

Keep on keeping on.

CHAPTER ELEVEN

Walking in the Shadows

*Even though I walk through the valley of the
shadow of death…*

—Psalm 23:4a

We have seen that the dark valley is a place where God does some of his most significant work in our lives. He hasn't left us. It's just the opposite. He is with us every step of the way. He is loving us. He is comforting us. He is refining us, making us the sons and daughters he has intended from the beginning. As David's great psalm teaches us, we won't die in the place of darkness. Rather, it is a place where we come to know him more than ever as our very life and hope. What dies in the valley are our illusions of self-sufficiency and our plans for self-preservation.

Often our thoughts and feelings haven't fully grasped this reality. We have what seem like internal enemies that are determined to steer us off God's path and get us so bogged down that we barely know how to take the next step. This is especially true with a valley like depression. What are we to do with these foes? How do we handle the darkness? We must surrender our current situation to the Shepherd and choose to walk with him in the midst of the shadows.

A famous American businessman, James Cash Penney (yes, that J.C. Penney), spent most of his adult life in the darkness. Yet he made a decision early in his life to follow the Shepherd in the midst of his darkness. J.C. Penney surrendered the darkness in the valley to trust wholeheartedly in the Shepherd. He had already set up his retail store, but problems with his workers, enormous debt, and a troubling lack of customers were causing him to have crippling anxiety. His nervousness brought on a terrible case of shingles. One night he was so overcome with fear and trembling that he felt he would not live to the morning, and he checked himself into a hospital.

He spent his sleepless night writing farewell letters to his wife, his son, and his friends. As the sun rose, he heard singing from the hospital chapel. The words of the hymn were "No matter what may be the test, God will take care of you." He realized the depths of his own sin and selfishness, and he pictured in his mind the Lord Jesus crucified on the cross because of his sins, because he loved him.

He walked into the chapel and surrendered his fears and worries to the Lord. He committed himself to God's care and love. He felt like he had been let out of the dungeon and into the sunlight. That would become a daily way of life for J.C. Penney. What almost killed him ended up changing his faith and his life for the better. This is often God's way with his children. He takes us to the brink so we learn to rely on him and not ourselves. The apostle Paul described his own valley experience in these terms: *"Indeed, we felt that we had received the sentence of death. But that was to make us rely not on ourselves but on God who raises the dead"* (2 Cor. 1:9).

So what are some of the things we must surrender in the valley? What are the shadows of death that must be handed over to the Shepherd? Here are 10 common emotions and experiences of those who live with seasons of depression or just face periods of sadness.

1. Fear

We all face fear on some level. Some fear is good, of course. As children, we learned not to touch a hot stove or run out into the street. As teenagers (and as adults, if we're honest) we tended to fear what others might think of us. Once we grow up, these fears just keep coming—fear we won't have enough money, fear of loneliness, sickness, failure, success, and on and on it goes. Once the darkness of fear has overtaken the mind, the result can be paralyzing.

Thankfully, many of the things we fear never actually happen. So it can be helpful to remind ourselves of a definition/acronym for FEAR from author and pastor Mark Batterson: False Expectations Appearing Real.[1] It helps us see how useless our fears often are. In any case, the best way to fight fear is with a greater fear. We must learn the greatest fear in this life is the fear of the Lord, which is the beginning of wisdom, according to Proverbs 9:10. Only God can cast out all fear with his reassuring love for us, as John wrote in 1 John 4:18. Jesus put it in very stark terms in Matthew 10:28: *"And do not fear those who kill the body but cannot kill the soul. Rather fear him who can destroy both soul and body in hell."* These verses are a great reminder that the only way to fight fear is with a greater fear.

> **The only way to fight fear is with a greater fear.**

2. Worry

Mark Twain famously said, "I've had a lot of worries in my life, most of which never happened." Worry is a close cousin to fear. Our fears are the fuel for worry. If we keep feeding our fears, worry is inevitable. Worry has no expiration date if nothing is done to get rid of it. We have to make a conscious decision to throw it out of our lives by faith and with God's help. At least attempt to worry in order. So much of our time is spent worrying about the future when our concerns should be on the present day. Learning to worry in order can go a long way to help each day.

Worry contributes to depression and often results from it. Darkness often moves in like an ocean fog. It feels just like the word the Germans use for worry: *choking*. Worrying about when—and if—we'll ever come out of the darkness takes so much energy that it can make life feel like a living death. In those times, we have to hold tightly to the belief that God is bigger than our fears and worries. King David said he didn't fear evil—he didn't imagine the worst—because he knew the Lord was with him. The same Lord is with us today—in our lives as they currently are.

3. Anxiety

Martyn Lloyd-Jones argues from the text of Scripture that Timothy, Paul's protégé, suffered from paralyzing anxiety. You are in good company if you can identify with Timothy. Just hearing the word *anxiety* is enough to make most of us a little anxious. Anxiety is a close cousin of fear and worry, so what we've already said also applies to anxiety. Anxiety means to divide. It's another energy drainer because when we're anxious, our minds are trying to process multiple tracks simultaneously. We're being pulled in two directions, and each direction carries messages to the heart. If we go down the fear track, it won't be long before we experience some level of anxiety and possibly some physical manifestations of stress such as headaches or stomachaches. On the other hand, if we go down the faith track, our fears and worries will shrink compared to the magnitude of God's power and goodness. The result is that we will experience more life and peace. Practically speaking, it's a Spirit-empowered battle to learn to *"take every thought captive to obey Christ"* (2 Cor. 10:5).

4. Discouragement

For many, depression is the direct result of discouragement and loss. They can be almost synonymous. A depressed person is almost certainly discouraged, and a discouraged person is extremely susceptible to depression. Take the person who has lost a job and is having trouble finding a new one in the field. The discouragement this man feels can very easily lead to deep depression if not constantly battled against.

Discouragement has a way of taking over our lives, darkening even the brightest day. When we're discouraged because of painful, unfulfilled longings or losses, we tend to see everything through the lens of the things we lack or have lost. So often our identities and plans for happiness are closely wrapped up with particular circumstances or outcomes, and when we don't get what we want, we can get discouraged. Part of the "severe mercy" of discouragement and depression is that it can show us more of ourselves and our idols, teaching us to find our happiness in God alone. This is easier said than done, of course, and hence the necessary battle to fight discouragement with faith.

One day the devil was auctioning off his tools. He had a high price on them all: pride, laziness, arrogance, hate, envy, jealousy. But there was one tool with a sign under it that read "Not for Sale." It was a strange-looking tool, which led someone to ask, "What is that tool and why isn't it for sale?" Satan answered, "I can't afford to get rid of that one! That's my chief tool: discouragement. With this tool, I can pry open a heart, and once I'm there, I can do most anything I want." When it comes to using discouragement against us, the devil plays for keeps. His goal, as always, is to damage our relationship with God, the ultimate source of encouragement and hope.

5. Despair

Despair is an extreme form of discouragement. It's like the person who said, "I was going to read a book on positive thinking, but then I thought, what good would that do?" Many have found themselves in situations where life has become crushingly difficult. When that happens, almost all hope departs from the heart and the mind. There appears to be neither a way out of the situation nor a way through it. When somebody says, "I'm at the end of my rope," they're speaking the language of despair. They desperately need a lifeline from God.

Despair can only be fought by crying out to God and asking him to help us renew our minds. God has created us to only have one thought at a time. So we fight despair by disciplining our minds to think on faith-strengthening truths about God and his character. For example, in Philippians 4:8, Paul encourages us to shift our thinking to focus on God's activity in the world and in our lives:

> *Finally, brothers, whatever is true, whatever is honorable, whatever is just, whatever is pure, whatever is lovely, whatever is commendable, if there is any excellence, if there is anything worthy of praise, think about these things.*

While only God and his truth can lift us from the depths of despair, God often uses our brothers and sisters in Christ to encourage us and sustain us when we feel particularly weak and hopeless. Our friends can be like the men who lowered the paralytic through the roof so he could receive a healing word from Jesus (Mark 2:1–12). In other words, there are times when we need to rely on the help of others to get out of the pit of despair.

6. Failure

A sense of personal failure is where the path of discouragement and despair often leads. It's also the great fear of so many people. What if I fail? Or worse, what if others know I have failed and therefore I am a failure? When we internalize a sense of failure, it feels as if we have the scarlet letter *F* emblazoned on our foreheads. Again, the battleground for this is in the mind. We must realize that failure is not final. God's amazing grace, mercy, and

> When we internalize a sense of failure, it feels as if we have the scarlet letter F emblazoned on our foreheads.

love are the lifters of our heads so we can see above our personal failings and trust that the Shepherd will lead us to green pastures. We must never forget the Shepherd is for us, not against us. Though we may fail, we are not failures. We are what God declares us to be: loved, chosen, redeemed, ransomed, purchased, saved, and soon-to-be glorified.

I know there are many—maybe you—who are in the darkness of depression, battling with the feeling of being a failure. You feel you have failed because you cannot fix yourself. Failure (or even perceived failure, which is probably just as common) not only often leads to depression, but it's frequently made worse by depression. That is, depression can lead to additional failures and the sense of *being* a failure. It can be a vicious cycle.

Consider our earlier example of the person who lost their job and was discouraged about it. This person, unless their identity is firmly rooted in Christ, will likely feel like a failure, which could affect everything they do going forward until the experience is reframed in light of the gospel and God's grace. Sadly, so many people who have lost a job have committed suicide because they can't shake the pervasive sense of failure that haunts their every step.

Satan, the accuser, aims to use our failures to make us feel disqualified from further service to God. He may not be able to prevent us from reaching heaven, but he will do everything in his power to destroy our effectiveness and joy on earth. A Christian who fails forward, so to speak, has learned to shut down Satan's accusations and connect their life to Christ's. The apostle Paul said, "*I do not even judge myself* " (1 Cor. 4:3). Are you judging yourself as a hopeless failure? Instead, look to Christ for your validation, worth, and potential, not the pronouncements of the devil, the world, or even yourself.

7. Anger

I have always said that if you want to see what is inside something, just bump it and see what spills out. When people are bumped in life, what seems to spill out most often is anger. This anger stems from pride with thoughts such as "I don't deserve to be treated this way; in fact, I deserve to be treated better than most." Another less obvious but perhaps more insidious form of pride takes the form of self-deprecation and a poor-me mentality. This mentality becomes a self-fulfilling prophecy: "See, I really deserved this poor treatment," we tell anyone who will listen.

We must remember that Christ was bumped often, even bearing the unfair agony of the cross, and yet he said, *"Father, forgive them, for they know not what they do"* (Luke 23:34). The anger we don't let go of through forgiveness can turn to bitterness, and bitterness is like an acid that will eat away its own container. Anger does not enhance judgment. Forfeiting our right to anger makes us deny ourselves.

Before moving on, I need to say a bit more about the link between unforgiving and depression. We've already noted how our anger usually stems from our pride. Similarly, the unforgiving spirit we lug around with us is connected to our pride.

The more we can grasp how much we've been forgiven in Christ, the easier it will be for us to let go of our anger and give others a little grace. One of the surest ways to stay depressed is to refuse to forgive others as we've been forgiven. For that matter, we need to let go of the anger and unforgiveness we feel toward ourselves. Depression has often been called anger turned inward, and that is no doubt true.

If God can forgive us—and really, only he can—we can certainly let ourselves off the hook for our sins and failures if we've confessed, repented, and made restitution where possible. In this regard, we don't need to hold ourselves to a higher standard than God does!

Have you ever thought about why Jesus had to suffer like he did?

We know he had to die to atone for our sins, but why the suffering? Why not just come, live, die, and be raised to life?

I believe it was to teach us about forgiveness. Remember what he said to the Father on the cross after being tortured, beaten, and shamed? *"Father, forgive them, for they know not what they do*" (Luke 23:34). Jesus is telling us that if God the Father can forgive them for what they did to his Son, then we can forgive the people who have hurt us. And since God has forgiven us, we can also forgive ourselves. Jesus suffered so we could learn to forgive like he forgives.

8. Isolation

After God created the heavens and the earth, he called everything good (Gen. 1:31). However, just a chapter later, in Genesis 2:18, God said, "*It is not good that the man should be alone.*" This comment by our Creator gives great insight into the nature of life according to God's design—it is relational through and through. God himself is a triune community of perfect love and fellowship. How could his plan for his people be otherwise?

Depression thrives in loneliness and isolation. Sometimes when we feel down, we don't feel like bringing others down with us. We're embarrassed and ashamed that we feel the way we do, so we foolishly keep it to ourselves, not realizing that reaching out

> **Depression thrives in loneliness and isolation.**

to others actually gives them the opportunity to love us, which they, being made in God's image, were designed to do. We can't bear each other's burdens if they're not made known.

The cost of loneliness and isolation can be huge. Prolonged, unattended loneliness and isolation diminish accountability, shrivel hope, and weaken our sense of purpose. To make matters worse, our loneliness and isolation often lead to poor judgment and giving in to temptation as a way to try to assuage the pain we feel. So we must recognize that while we're in the dark shadows of depression, it will feel natural to isolate ourselves and avoid others. The solution is to pursue what doesn't feel natural. We must move toward people and seek out godly, Christ-centered relationships despite how we feel.

9. Hopelessness

It's a common saying that human beings can live for 40 days without food, four days without water, and four minutes without air. But we can't live for four seconds without hope.

> **Human beings can live for 40 days without food, four days without water, and four minutes without air. But we can't live for four seconds without hope.**

That is very true. Think back to the scene in the Garden of Eden after the curse. What did God give to Adam and Eve and, by extension, to all of us? He gave us *hope*. When cursing the serpent, he promised in Genesis 3:15, "*I will put enmity between you and the woman, and between your offspring and her offspring; he shall bruise your head, and you shall bruise his heel.*" Even in the midst of the hopelessness of sin and the curse, there was the promised hope of the Messiah someday crushing sin, Satan, and all of his shadowy schemes. We must learn to take God at his word and know that as we follow the Shepherd, our best days are ahead of us. In light of eternity, we are nowhere near past our prime. Our true life with Christ has barely begun. Our future is incredibly bright.

Of course, depression tells us that things are hopeless and are unlikely to ever change. Depression is a liar, though. God's specialty is bringing hope to seemingly hopeless situations. The fact that we often can't predict when and how he'll deliver us doesn't mean that he won't. The Bible is full of stories of God's gracious intervention in the lives of his people in ways they never could have imagined. We can trust God. We really can. Hope, not hopelessness, will have the last word because God is with us, and he loves us with an unending, unstoppable love. Our God is the God of all hope (Romans 15:13). So we must never, ever give up hope.

10. Numbness

The loss of feeling, the sense of numbness that can accompany depression, is a leprosy of the soul. Missionary doctor Paul Brand, whose work with lepers is legendary, explained leprosy this way:

> [Leprosy] only numbs the extremities. The destruction of limbs follows solely because the warning system of pain is gone; so the routine of life takes its toll upon lepers by cuts, burns, bruises, sprains, broken bones, all without any consciousness by the leper that it has happened. Consequently, he continues with open, festering wounds, or limps on twisted legs, and gradually becomes disfigured and repulsive to others.[2]

God created us to feel, both physically and emotionally. Feelings are warning signals for protection and often for direction. God heals our numbness through his presence and truth. With God's strength, we can choose to take the next right step of faith even when we're not feeling it. Many times, our emotions will follow our obedience. That is what a life of faith looks like—taking God at his word and walking forward with him into the future he has for us.

Where the battle rages

There is no medication that can ultimately remove all the foes we face in the darkness. The best that medication can do is help a person manage the symptoms of the darkness. Therefore, we must work hard to fight where we can the battle in our mind. The current Secretary of Defense, General James Mattis knows firsthand the challenges of the battlefield. He teaches his men this truth: "The most important six inches on the battlefield is between your ears."[3] This is a good message for us as we fight our own battle with the darkness.

> There is no medication that can ultimately remove all the foes we face in the darkness. The best that medication can do is help a person manage the symptoms of the darkness. Therefore, we must work hard to fight where we can the battle in our mind.

Each of these foes seeks to devour our souls. We must fight back. The battle is a daily one; for some, like Charles Spurgeon, it is a lifetime one. The key is learning that in the darkness, there is life and hope. We must learn to walk through the darkness, not give in to it.

> The most important six inches on the battlefield is between your ears.

The battle to find light in the darkness could be short for some; for others, it is lifelong and will require an adjustment to a person's perspective. The people of Tromsø might help with perspective. They have learned to do life in physical darkness. Tromsø is a tiny island of Norway located more than 200 miles north of the Arctic Circle. It is roughly the same size as Manhattan and has approximately 70,000 inhabitants, making it the second-most populated city north of the Arctic Circle.

Tromsø is home to extreme light variation between seasons.

During the polar night, which lasts from November to January, the sun doesn't rise at all. Then the days get progressively longer until the midnight sun period, from May to July, when the sun never sets. After the midnight sun, the days get shorter and shorter again until the polar night and the yearly cycle repeats.

The people of Tromsø have learned that life is seasonal, and that darkness is expected.

They have learned to live with periods of darkness rather than look for immediate ways to escape the inevitable. Interestingly, many find peace, life, and even joy in those long winters of no light. We can as well. It's not easy, but neither are we alone and without direction. There is One

> The people of Tromsø have learned that life is seasonal, and that darkness is expected.

who loves us, is always with us, and always guides us. As David affirms in Psalm 36:9, *"In your light do we see light."* Your life may not have the light, but David found that God's light is always on, and that may be the only light available. Look to the light and keep looking one day at a time for as long as it takes.

Are you going to live with and fight against depression your whole life?

Maybe. Maybe not.

But instead of fighting off the darkness, maybe God wants to provide the daily mercies to live with the darkness in the light of his grace. Darkness could be your thorn, but it can become your friend, not just your foe.

Let the darkness pass over.

Wait for the sunrise.

Keep hope alive.

CHAPTER TWELVE

A Theology of "Withness"

I will fear no evil, for you are with me;
your rod and your staff, they comfort me.

—Psalm 23:4b

Years ago, when our kids were smaller, we would take them to Chuck E. Cheese's. These "fun" family excursions amounted to adult purgatory, but that is for another book. I can remember a time there with our oldest daughter, Natalie, when she was three or four years old. She was completely engrossed in one of their countless games. As she played, I moved back toward our table where I could still see her and keep my eye on her.

When she had finished the game, she turned around to look at me and discovered I was gone. If panic has a face, I saw it that day. She was all alone, or so she thought. Not only was I very close, but I could even see the tears running down her cheek. I quickly moved toward her to assure her of my presence. In my arms, she questioned and scolded me for leaving her all alone. I tried to explain to her that I was right there close by, that she never left my sight, and that she was extremely loved and safe the whole time. The problem was that not one of her five senses informed her mind or her heart that I was present and that she was safe. She could not see, hear, feel, smell, or taste my presence.

When our natural senses do not provide the security we long for, we must set our minds on the truth of the Scriptures. Just because you sometimes *feel* alone does not mean you actually *are* alone.

Never alone

One of the greatest fears in life for many people is to be left all alone. This might even be a huge part of your dark valley experience. The fear of aloneness can bring a tsunami of negative emotions, engulfing the heart and mind. God said it is not good for man to be alone because it's not. He made us; he knows. We were made for connection with him and with others. This is especially true in tough times. All the "one another" commands in the New Testament assume that Christians are living in community with other believers. For various reasons, we nevertheless sometimes feel alone.

Thankfully, some of the best news for those going through a dark valley of discouragement, despair, or depression is that *you are not alone*—ever! That's the biblical truth of the matter. David wrote in Psalm 23:4, "*I will fear no evil, for you are with me.*" Notice that David did not write "there is no evil." He sees life under the sun as a place where there is real evil. There are real threats to our security. But he quickly reminded himself (and us) that we are not alone. The Good Shepherd is always with us. In fact, God's presence, the reality of "you are with me" might be the most comforting truth in the entire Bible. To know that our Shepherd is with us in the darkness is probably the greatest thing we can know, because it speaks hope to us. When we are walking in darkness, we desperately need hope. God's presence provides that hope, unlike anything else.

Consider what Jesus said to his disciples in his Great Commission charge in Matthew 28:20: "And behold, I am with you always, to the end of the age." Then combine that with the promise of the Shepherd in Hebrews 13:5—"*I will never leave you nor forsake you*"—and you can see that God is always with us; there is no chance of abandonment. But what about when life's circumstances are really difficult? What then? What about when it seems as if we're on our own? The apostle Paul had something to say about that in Romans 8:37–39:

> *No, in all these things we are more than conquerors through him who loved us. For I am sure that neither death nor life, nor angels nor rulers, nor things present nor things to come, nor powers, nor height nor depth, nor anything else in all creation, will be able to separate us from the love of God in Christ Jesus our Lord.*

The rock-solid truth of the Bible is that you are not alone. You are *never* alone. No matter what is happening in your life right now, the Good Shepherd has not left you. You may sin and get yourself into trouble, but he doesn't abandon you—ever! Rest assured, if his eye is on the sparrow—and it is—then surely, he has not taken his eye off of you.

Safe and secure

The Good Shepherd provides the safety we need in two ways—protection and correction. Without protection, we could get hurt by things outside of our control. Without correction, we could hurt ourselves through our own foolishness and poor decisions. So David concluded Psalm 23:4 by saying, "*Your rod and your staff, they comfort me.*"

A shepherd carried a rod with him to defend himself and the flock. This was a club-like instrument with a metal tip on the end. It was used to protect the flock from predators such as wolves, coyotes, cougars, or stray dogs. The shepherd would fend off these enemies of the sheep from the many dangers the sheep faced. Without his protection, the sheep wouldn't last long; without our Shepherd's protection, we won't last long, either.

The prophet Isaiah said we are all like sheep who have gone astray (Isa. 53:6). In other words, we make bad choices; we do dumb things; we get ourselves into trouble. In our times of wandering, we expose ourselves to danger. Nevertheless, just a chapter later, Isaiah wrote:

> No weapon that is fashioned against you shall succeed, and you shall refute every tongue that rises against you in judgment. This is the heritage of the servants of the Lord and their vindication from me, declares the Lord.
>
> —Isaiah 54:17

Ultimately, our safety and security are dependent on the grace of the Shepherd looking out for us. It is not the result of our careful planning and anxious efforts to control everything in our lives. We simply are not capable of protecting ourselves.

Correction and guidance

David also said that a shepherd carries a staff. A shepherd's staff was made out of wood, usually with a hook or curved top. The staff was used to correct, lift, guide, steer, and rescue the sheep. The staff, like the rod, would not be necessary if the sheep had their act together and were totally self-sufficient creatures. Clearly, that was (and is) not the case. Despite delusions of self-sufficiency, we're no better off than sheep when it comes to handling what life throws at us. We're not up to the task. In fact, a large part of sanctification, of growing in grace, is learning just how dependent we really are.

Here's the thing: God doesn't want spoiled kids any more than we want them. So he takes it upon himself to correct our wrong ways of thinking and living before we self-destruct. His correction is actually a great mercy. Listen to Hebrews 12:7-11:

> *It is for discipline that you have to endure. God is treating you as sons. For what son is there whom his father does not discipline? If you are left without discipline, in which all have participated, then you are illegitimate children and not sons. Besides this, we have had earthly fathers who disciplined us and we respected them. Shall we not much more be subject to the Father of spirits and live? For they disciplined us for a short time as it seemed best to them, but he disciplines us for our good, that we may share his holiness. For the moment all discipline seems painful rather than pleasant, but later it yields the peaceful fruit of righteousness to those who have been trained by it.*

We tend to think of discipline as a negative, but it's actually a positive in the hands of God. God disciplines all his children for their good, though it doesn't always feel good at the time. Of course, we're not wise enough to know what we need, which is a big part of our problem. God, being all-wise and all-loving, is willing to allow pain in our lives for the greater purpose of growing us in wisdom and holiness. He wants us to experience the "peaceful fruit of righteousness," which is worth more than all the pain it takes to get there.

Not too long ago, I saw a quote on Facebook that said, "I was spanked as a kid and now I have a disorder called respect for authority." Purposeful discipline is a loving gift to the recipient. Sowing seeds of discipline now results in a harvest of righteousness later. Of course, it is hard to understand at the time—"for the moment all discipline seems painful rather than pleasant"—but by faith we must choose to trust God's plan.

What it comes down is our view of God. Do we view God as wise and loving, or do we suspect that he doesn't always know what he's doing and might even hold a grudge against us because of our sins and failures? Charles Spurgeon said it so well: "God is too good to be unkind and he is too wise to be mistaken. And when we cannot trace his hand, we must trust his heart."[1]

Even in the dark times, even in the pit of depression, God is up to something good in your life.

He has not abandoned you; he is with you.

He will help you.

Trust it to be so.

CHAPTER THIRTEEN

Welcomed and Blessed

*You prepare a table before me in the presence
of my enemies; you anoint my head with oil;
my cup overflows.*

—Psalm 23:5

Are you a half-full or half-empty person?

At one time or another, we've all been asked if our proverbial glass is half empty or half full. But how we see our glass is a matter of perspective. Technically, it's both, but how we answer is supposed to reveal whether we're an optimist or a pessimist at heart. That's fine, as far as it goes, but I don't want to live my Christian life on a half-empty or half-full basis.

The cup of blessing

In Psalm 23:5, David described his cup as *overflowing*. He saw his walk with God as expanding beyond the normal limits of good fortune to an overflowing experience of God's grace. In effect, he was saying something like this: "When I live my life before God, my Shepherd, he provides me a cup of blessing that's not half empty or half full, but overflowing."

David saw his capacity not in terms of himself but in terms of his Shepherd. The apostle Paul told the church at Corinth that God said to him, *"My grace is sufficient for you, for my power is made perfect in weakness"* (2 Cor. 12:9). Pastor Alistair Begg reminds us that this means weakness is a distinct advantage in the Christian life. David didn't look at his ability; he looked at who God is and what God can do. He knew that God's desire was for him to live a life that was overflowing, although it would not necessarily be an easy life, a pain-free life, a money-rich life, or a sickness-free life. The love and goodness of God, and nothing else, is what makes our lives overflow with blessing.

We might think it would be easy for a king like David to have an overflowing cup, but that's not necessarily the case. David had to learn to trust God just like we do. As a young boy, David was out in the fields shepherding sheep when he learned that God would shepherd him. In facing many dangers, he learned to rely on God and not himself. He learned that while his capacity was limited, God's was not.

A case in point is David's confrontation with Goliath. David arrived on the scene to see the giant Goliath mocking the Israelites and challenging someone to fight him. Goliath even mocked the Israelites' God, which was too much for David. Since nobody would stand up to Goliath, David took it upon himself to do so. He knew that the battle was really the Lord's, not his, so he was unafraid of the giant. He felled Goliath with a precisely aimed stone and then finished the job by cutting off his head, just as he said he would. David showed up to the battle, but God gave him the victory.

What we learn from this episode in David's life is that our view of God is key to our trusting him and acting in faith. The truth is, how we view God impacts everything about our Christian life. Renowned 20th-century pastor and author A. W. Tozer put it his way: "What comes into our minds when we think about God is the most important thing about us."[1] If we don't understand the character of God, we will be hesitant to trust him, and we will suffer unnecessary pain for our lack of faith. On the other hand, if we understand who God is, we will understand that he is with us even through the dark valleys of life.

> "What comes into our minds when we think about God is the most important thing about us."

Here's a quick diagnostic. When we're exhausted physically or emotionally, there's a good chance it's because we're living out of a half-empty or a half-full glass, trying desperately to manage life with our own limited capacity. That never works for long. Both our successes and failures will deplete us if it's just *us* we're relying upon to make life work. While being an optimist is usually better than being a pessimist, it's not enough. We need to be realists about our capacity as well as God's capacity. The reason you can hope in the valley of depression and discouragement is simply because you plus God make up a profound majority. He fills your cup.

> While being an optimist is usually better than being a pessimist, it's not enough. We need to be realists about our capacity as well as God's capacity.

The bottom line is that if we're not depending on God, our cup will run empty very quickly. Our country has a Declaration of Independence. We can go see this highly esteemed document in a glass enclosure. Psalm 23 is also a declaration of dependence that says we can trust God and not ourselves.

The table of provision

In Psalm 23:5, David wrote, "You prepare a table before me," which is remarkable if you think about it. God Almighty, the Creator of the universe, the one who formed and fashioned me in my mother's womb, is daily preparing a table before me. Not only that, he does it in the presence of my *enemies*. Having enemies doesn't mean God is absent; he's especially present when we're facing enemies. Just remembering that can be a depression lifter.

A good shepherd takes care of his sheep, including leading them to food and water. Think of God's table as a Princess Cruise buffet, not mere army rations. Have you ever been on a floating buffet? It just never ends; it's 24/7. If you wake up at 3:00 a.m. and want mashed potatoes, they've got them. Like an endless, always-open buffet, God is our ever-present, always-available provider. Everything you have is from the gracious hand of God— your house, your possessions, your friends, your family, your church, everything.

We've all had the experience of enjoying a great meal that a friend or family member has prepared for us. We recognize the thoughtfulness and effort that went into it. We feel very loved by the person who has gone to such trouble for us. We feel very cared for. Our God treats us with that kind of generosity and hospitality every single day, although we tend to take his provisions for granted. When we pray the Lord's Prayer, asking for our daily bread, we should do so with expectation and gratitude, rather than doubt and entitlement.

God's table is bountiful. It overflows with blessings. Of course, depression and despair whisper to us that we don't have enough or that God won't provide. Neither is true. When people ask me how I'm doing, I often reply, "Better than I deserve." And that's the truth in light of the table of blessings and provisions God prepares for me every day.

Like making preparations for a good home-cooked meal, the shepherd goes to great lengths to provide just what his sheep need. The greater his sacrifice, the greater the demonstration of his love. In ancient Israel, the best feeding grounds were often located on a mountain. There were some flat ridges in the mountains that came to the very edge of water. A shepherd could hike and find these spots for the sheep to graze and get a drink. Sometimes it took hours to get there. We might compare the sacrifice the shepherd made to our going on a long trip with little kids in the car. They get hungry and irritable. Sheep get that way, too. Sheep even sometimes bite. Yet the shepherd takes them where they need to go, no matter how inconvenient it is for him.

> **Find a seat at the table he prepared for you.**

Find a seat at the table he prepared for you.

The reality of enemies

Anyone who has suffered with depression knows that we have enemies in this life; we walk through dark valleys. That's why we must understand that God is with us in the presence of our enemies. They don't all disappear as much as we'd like them to. Our Shepherd wants us to trust him no matter what we're going through.

In Israel, the adder snake is a deadly enemy of sheep. These snakes hide in little holes in the ground, and when the sheep are grazing, the snake pokes its head out and bites the sheep on the nose, injecting its poison and killing the sheep. Knowing the danger, a good Shepherd will walk the grazing land before the sheep arrive and find every little hole where an adder could be. The shepherd will take some type of oil or grease and put it on the edges of the hole so when the adder tries to poke its head out, it slips back down and it is not able to bite the sheep. Then the shepherd will call all of his sheep by name, inviting them to come graze without fear of harm while in the presence of their enemies.

Your enemies might not be snakes; they might look more like a boss or someone who gives you a hard time about your faith. Don't see depression, discouragement, and despair as the enemy. The enemy is sin and Satan. He is the worst enemy of all. Both seek to paralyze you in the darkness so you can't take the step of faith.

The apostle Paul warns us about one of these enemies:

> *Be sober-minded; be watchful. Your adversary the devil prowls around like a roaring lion, seeking someone to devour.*
>
> —1 Peter 5:8

That verse says we are being hunted by the enemy. Paul also helps us understand the nature of the battle:

> *For we do not wrestle against flesh and blood, but against the rulers, against the authorities, against the cosmic powers over this present darkness, against the spiritual forces of evil in the heavenly places.*
>
> —Ephesians 6:12

Unfortunately, most of us don't take the devil and spiritual warfare as seriously as we should. Rather than being sober-minded, we tend to be oblivious. And rather than fighting against our spiritual enemy, we tend to fight against other people.

We must understand that Jesus may not remove all of our enemies right away, but he will help us deal with them. So when we experience challenges in our marriages or parenting or friendships, we must recognize that the other person is not the enemy. The enemy is behind the scenes, trying to cause conflict and distrust, and trying to get us depressed and angry at God. We must not fall for his schemes. The truth is, we can't avoid all conflict in our marriages or protect our kids from all the evil that's in the world, but we can trust Jesus to be with us to provide what we need to keep going.

Think of David. He certainly had his share of enemies. He was often at odds with his own family. Other nations were after him because they were enemies of Israel. King Saul became insanely jealous of him and tried to kill him on multiple occasions. Certainly, Uriah's family had plenty against David. Despite all of his troubles and enemies, David knew the Lord was with him, and he trusted the Lord to provide what he needed.

How to deal with enemies

Romans 12 gives some incredibly helpful guidelines for dealing with enemies. Verses 17 and 18 say:

> *Repay no one evil for evil, but give thought to do what is honorable in the sight of all. If possible, so far as it depends on you, live peaceably with all.*

So step one is to *rethink* how we've been responding to our enemies. We are not to pay people back for what they have done to us; instead, we are to seek peace with them. We are to "give thought" to our reactions, knowing that others are watching how we respond. We are either representing Christ well by responding in this way or we are following our flesh and the ways of the world and adding fuel to the fire. Guess which path leads to peace and which one leads to turmoil and contributes to depression? Christianity is

> **Christianity is best seen not in how we act, but in how we react.**

best seen not in how we act, but in how we react.

The next step in dealing with our enemies in a godly way is to *release* them from our wrath and foolish plans for revenge. Romans 12:19 says:

> *Beloved, never avenge yourselves, but leave it to the wrath of God, for it is written, "Vengeance is mine, I will repay, says the Lord."*

That verse doesn't leave us any wiggle room. It says, "Never avenge yourselves." We must trust God to right every wrong we experience in this life. We might not receive complete justice in

> **Forgiveness is to let go of our hope for a different or better past.**

this life, but we can trust God to make things right in the end. Forgiveness is to let go of our hope for a different or better past. It's giving up your right to get even.

Finally, we are to *return* evil with good. That's the most radical step of all. Let's look at Romans 12:20–21:

> *"If your enemy is hungry, feed him; if he is thirsty, give him something to drink; for by so doing you will heap burning coals on his head." Do not be overcome by evil, but overcome evil with good.*

This is hard to do; it is not natural to respond this way. But we're called to live a supernatural, God-empowered life, not a natural life. When you live your life knowing that God is your provider, the commands to *rethink* your response, *release* your wrath and desire for revenge, and *return* good to your enemy make a whole lot more sense and result in a whole lot more peace.

The Shepherd cares for you

God not only provides for us, but he also cares for us. He is our caregiver. Have you ever read Isaiah 43? It's a real blessing of a passage. God basically told Israel something like this: "I know it's hard right now, but I love you, and I'm going to take care of you." You may not feel this truth right now, so you might need to speak truth to your heart despite how you feel. The truth is that God is not against you. If you follow Jesus Christ, he is your Lord and Savior. He's for you; he loves you; he wants to care for you.

> You anoint my head with oil.

David spoke of God's care when he said, *"You anoint my head with oil"* (Ps. 23:5).

Picture that lamb in the lap of the shepherd. He gently works the oil into the skin of the lamb. It brings relief. It brings comfort. It brings healing. We don't use oil that much today, but people do get massages where the therapist applies oil to tired, stressed-out muscles. There's great care happening during a massage. That's what David was communicating—that he felt deeply cared for by God despite going through dark valleys and facing many enemies.

There were two ways the shepherd used oil to care for his sheep. The first way was to ward off pesky flies. Flies could make sheep miserable, particularly in the summer.

Sometimes flies would work their way into the sheep's nasal cavity and cause it a lot of pain. A shepherd would anoint the sheep's head with oil because it served as an effective fly repellent.

Sheep could also get a disease called scab. It would grow on the head of one sheep and then spread to the others. When a sheep got scab, the shepherd would gather that sheep into his lap and anoint him with oil to bring healing and prevent the further spread of the misery.

This beautiful line in David's great psalm reveals just how deeply God cares for us. He will intimately and graciously anoint us with oil, so to speak, and heal us and care for us. If you are depressed right now, know that God cares about you. Know that he sees you and loves you. Know that he desires to heal you and will heal you substantially in this life and completely in the life to come. Let this picture of his gentleness and care shape your view of him and your suffering.

Consider another picture of God's care from the Scriptures. In Matthew 6, Jesus said that if God cares for the lilies of the field (which he does), then he will certainly take care of you. That's a pretty good argument. God treats

> David is saying that God is not someone to question; he's someone to follow.

his people well; he doesn't neglect us. Even when he disciplines us, it's for our ultimate good. He does it because he cares for us, not because he doesn't.

David is saying that God is not someone to question; he's someone to follow. God is not someone to doubt; he's someone to trust. God is not someone to fear; he's somebody to rest in. He's our Good Shepherd. He's not some disengaged deity.

When we begin to see God as he really is, our capacity changes, which is another way of saying our faith grows. Our perspective is no longer half empty or half full, but overflowing with hope and potential. Why? Because we know that God is for us, not against us. He's our provider and our caregiver.

He is pouring overflowing grace into our lives every single day, grace that's more than enough to sustain us through the dark valley of depression, grace that's enough to defeat the enemy and bring relief from our depression one day at a time.

The Good Shepherd cares for us because he really cares about us.

Be still.

Rest in his sovereign care.

Let him fill your cup.

CHAPTER FOURTEEN

Unstoppable Love, Unshakable Hope

*Surely goodness and mercy shall follow me all
the days of my life, and I shall dwell in the house
of the Lord forever.*

—Psalm 23:6

185

Psalm 23 is enormously popular for good reason—it speaks beautifully to the needs of the human soul with a perfect economy of words. The psalm is like a glass elevator giving the reader great views of the Good Shepherd. The last verse of this magnificent psalm is especially helpful for dealing with depression as it offers additional perspective and unshakable hope. Depression has a way of shrinking our world to just us and our earthbound problems. Psalm 23 expands our world to the size of God and eternity.

In the previous chapter, we saw how God's blessings overflow in our lives even when we're going through hard times. His presence with us is the greatest blessing of all, and it is not lessened or eliminated by dark valleys and enemies. It is not lessened or eliminated by depression.

The truth is that living in this world is difficult, and dealing with depression is hard. It's no use pretending that things are easier or better than they are. But there's also no reason, if you're a Christian, to give in to the darkness. This final verse in Psalm 23 is a giant exclamation point on God's faithfulness, goodness, love, and mercy, both now and forever, in the lives of all his people. As such, it is a declaration of hope, and if there's anything the depressed person needs, it's hope.

The big picture

I'm not a photography expert, but I understand that there are basically two types of lenses: a telephoto lens and a wide-angle lens. A telephoto lens lets you focus on something small so that it looks big. Too often, I see my life's circumstances through a telephoto lens. I dial in so closely on a situation that it becomes all I can see. I lose all perspective about everything else; I'm not even aware of what else is going on.

Psalm 23 can help us remove the telephoto lens we've grown accustomed to using and replace it with a wide-angle lens. This wide-angle lens enables us to step back and gain some much-needed perspective about our lives. We see the forest through the trees; we see the big picture, and we see that there's no reason to panic when things aren't going well. With a wide-angle lens, God is included in the frame, whereas before, he was almost entirely outside the picture.

Pursued by goodness

David wisely reminded himself of God's faithfulness. We must do the same, especially when we're feeling depressed. The first half of Psalm 23:6 reads, "Surely goodness and mercy shall follow me all the days of my life." The first thing the wide-angle lens of this verse shows us is that we are being *pursued* by the Shepherd. God Almighty is pursuing us to perfect us, not to punish us. Remember, our cups are overflowing with his blessing. We're not half-empty or half-full people.

The Lord is our Shepherd, providing for us and taking care of us. Notice that the verse uses the word *surely* to describe God's pursuit of us. David is supremely confident that God has not abandoned him and never will. Some other translations use the word *only* to describe the nature of God's pursuit—*only goodness and mercy* follow us. Either way you translate it, it's more than a little encouraging.

Some objections might immediately spring to your mind in light of all the bad things that have happened to you in your life and in the lives of those you love. The reality is that we live in a fallen world, and bad things happen to us and to everyone we know. In fact, all of us will die at some point, which would seem to be the worst thing possible. The suffering we experience in this life in no way negates the truth of this verse. Instead, it serves as a reminder that we need to see life through the wide-angle lens of God and eternity.

Even death, the last enemy, was defeated by Christ (1 Cor. 15:26). The apostle Paul said to die and be with Christ is far better than life on earth (Phil. 1:23). Death for a Christian is the entryway to eternal bliss in the presence of God. So even when we die, we live. That perspective makes the tough times more manageable. C. S. Lewis put it this way: "If you think of this world as a place intended simply for our happiness, you find it quite intolerable: think of it as a place for training and correction and it's not so bad."[1] We need to take the long-term view. Our last day on earth will be our very best day.

> **Our last day on earth will be our very best day.**

Think of Lazarus. Jesus raised him from the dead, but guess what happened to him after that? He eventually died again. Even so, Jesus said to the crowd by Lazarus' tomb in John 11:25–26:

> *"I am the resurrection and the life. Whoever believes in me, though he die, yet shall he live, and everyone who lives and believes in me shall never die. Do you believe this?"*

If we believe this—and we have every reason to take the word of a man who predicted his own death and resurrection and then pulled it off—then we needn't fear death or the worst life can throw at us. For a Christian, death is not a demotion, but a promotion. To be absent from the body is to be present with the Lord. In the meantime, goodness and mercy will follow us all of our days here on planet Earth. That's the wide-angle view.

Let's take it a little further and really drive the point home. The Hebrew word translated *follow* is *radaph*. It is a hunting term and means to chase down. It literally means to be pursued or chased. God is in hot pursuit of us. I've been known to tailgate another driver on occasion, though I assure my wife that I'm just drafting to save gas. Unconvinced, she often observes that our bumpers were almost connected. That's how close God is to us. He is tailgating us with his goodness and mercy. You may not see him—he may be in your blind spot—but he is right there pursuing you all the way. David said in Psalm 139:5:

You hem me in, behind and before.

We couldn't shake God and his love and mercy even if we wanted to.

I also spent about 16 hours studying the Hebrew word translated *goodness*, and you know what it means? It simply means goodness. Not the best use of my time. Actually, we can say a little bit more about it. Goodness relates to the Hebrew idea of *shalom*, meaning peace, welfare, completeness, or success. Basically, we would want as much goodness in our lives as we could possibly get. And the really great news is that God is absolutely determined to give it to us. He is chasing after us with his goodness, all day, every day, even when it doesn't seem like it. Again, we are called to trust what we can't see;

> Faith is the one thing God most wants from us. He is most honored by our faith.

faith is a must-have for any spiritual victories we hope to experience. Faith is the one thing God most wants from us. He is most honored by our faith.

Chased by mercy

The word translated *mercy* in Psalm 23:6 is the Hebrew word *hesed*. It's used 246 times in the Old Testament. Sometimes translated *steadfast love*, it's God's loving-kindness toward his people. It refers to God's covenantal love with the nation Israel and also his covenantal love mediated through Jesus Christ in the new covenant.

Incidentally, the word *covenant* means "to cut," which relates to the shedding of blood. The new covenant was established through the blood of Jesus Christ; covenant love is sacrificial love. The Lord doesn't just tell us about his love; he demonstrates it—supremely through the sacrifice of Jesus but also through every other blessing we receive from his hand.

God's mercy, his steadfast love, and his covenant faithfulness are manifestations of his glory. They describe who he *is*. In Exodus 33:18, Moses said to God, *"Please show me your glory."* Remember, glory is what you are known for, as we discussed earlier. God honored Moses's request by describing who he is. Exodus 34:6 reads:

> *The Lord passed before him and proclaimed, "The Lord, the Lord, a God merciful and gracious, slow to anger, and abounding in steadfast love and faithfulness."*

God's glory is wrapped up in his mercy, in his steadfast love. Psalm 23 says he is chasing us with his merciful love. It is his glory to do so.

We can never go too far with the love of God. The love of God is a bottomless well; it just never runs out. We must preach a balanced message that God is holy and just, but that does not limit his love in the least. His love is a holy love, a just love. These two types of love are not in conflict. When you're discouraged, when you're depressed, you especially need to remember and believe that God is a lover, a forgiver, a reconciler, a redeemer, a purchaser. He doesn't hold a grudge; he's not angry at you. Instead,

> **You can never go too far with the love of God.**

he's a chaser, a pursuer, a giver, and an encourager. You can never go too far with the love of God.

God's love is stubborn, even relentless. When you confessed your sins and surrendered your life to the lordship of Jesus Christ, it was because God had already set his love upon you. Ephesians 1:4 says that *"he chose us in him before the foundation of the world."* God in eternity past set his *hesed* love upon us. If you know Jesus, you are God's beloved, and his pursuit of you is relentless. You were once the lost sheep in Jesus's parable, and he came after you. He still comes after you, even when you run from him and don't believe he loves you.

I believe the Bible teaches four concrete things about God's *hesed*, covenantal love. First, his love is *uninfluenced*. Consider God's tender words to Israel in Deuteronomy 7:7–8:

It was not because you were more in number than any other people that the Lord set his love on you and chose you, for you were the fewest of all peoples, but it is because the Lord loves you and is keeping the oath that he swore to your fathers, that the Lord has brought you out with a mighty hand and redeemed you from the house of slavery, from the hand of Pharaoh king of Egypt.

God basically said that he didn't choose them because they were awesome; quite the opposite, actually. His choice of Israel was uninfluenced by their qualifications or deserving. You can't influence the love of God in your life either. It's uninfluenced. He loves you because he wants to; end of story. This is very good news for people who constantly fail to live up to their own expectations, let alone what we imagine God requires of us for him to love us. When it comes to embracing and experiencing God's love, we can't rely on natural thinking. We have to trust what Gods says is true.

Second, God's love is *unconditional.* Romans 5:8 says, *"God shows his love for us in that while we were still sinners, Christ died for us."* When we were sinners, when we were enemies of God, when we were hostile to God in our minds, when we were dead in our trespasses, when we were alienated from God, when we would never choose Christ, God said, "I chose you. It's unconditional." That is what the Greeks called *agape* love, the love of choice and sacrifice. Pastor and

> Agape love is "giving someone what they need most, when they deserve it least, at great personal cost to yourself."

author Chip Ingram describes agape love this way: "Giving someone what they need most, when they deserve it least, at great personal cost to yourself."[2]

Unconditional love demonstrates strength on God's part because the stronger person in the relationship always initiates the peace, and the stronger person is God. It's his call, and he chooses to love us.

One more verse on this is Titus 3:5: "*He saved us, not because of works done by us in righteousness, but according to his own mercy.*" It can't get much clearer than that. God's love is unconditional, and that is more great news for people who can't seem to get everything right, no matter how hard they try.

Third, God's love is *unchanging.* James 1:17 says, "*Every good gift and every perfect gift is from above, coming down from the Father of lights, with whom there is no variation or shadow due to change.*" God doesn't change. God's love doesn't change either. This is so hard for us to understand because our love changes all the time based on how we feel. We've all seen relationships fall apart because love proved fickle, not faithful. God isn't like us, though, and his love isn't like our love. It's unchanging. In 1 John 4:8, it says, "*God is love.*" If God is love, then everything that's true about God is also true about his love, right? And what's true about God is that he is unchanging, just as James 1:17 says. God's love is as unchanging as his character — completely. This type of love is when a person says, "I have seen the worst parts of you, and I am staying."

The fourth thing we can say about God's love is that it is *unending.* Jeremiah 31:3 says, "*I have loved you with an everlasting love; therefore I have continued my faithfulness to you.*" We're loved with an everlasting love. That means it doesn't end, ever. It doesn't end when we sin; it doesn't end when we're depressed; it doesn't end, period. Your groceries may have a use-by date, but God's love doesn't. It's unending.

One of my favorite verses is Lamentations 3:22, "*The steadfast love of the Lord never ceases; his mercies never come to an end.*" That verse couldn't be clearer about the permanence of God's love and mercy. *Never* is an amplifying word. It amplifies the truth or untruth of something. When God speaks about his love and mercy, he has every right to use the word *never* in connection with the possibility of it ending because his love will never, ever end. He's pursuing us. He's chasing us. The hound of heaven is after us. Surely his goodness and mercy shall follow us all the days of our lives.

With God forever

The second half of Psalm 23:6 is what I call a "wasabi statement." It's a small sentence but has a big punch. It reads, "*And I shall dwell in the house of the Lord forever.*" The Hebrew text could also be translated, "I shall come back again and again to be present in the house of the Lord." Again, this verse teaches us to see things through the wide-angle lens of eternity rather than our present circumstances, whether good or bad.

What did David mean by "house of the Lord"? David wanted to build the temple, but God was going to leave that task to David's son Solomon. Nevertheless, the best was yet to come for David, as it is for us, too. As followers of Christ, remember that our best days are always ahead of us.

Depression frequently occurs after a big loss or a series of losses. Life can seem hopeless in the short term. That's why we must learn to look beyond the short term to our glorious future with God in heaven. Heaven is our ultimate hope.

In heaven, we will dwell with God forever; it is not a temporary escape or a fleeting experience like the best of times on earth. Our heavenly home is a permanent dwelling place.

> Heaven is our ultimate hope. In heaven, we will dwell with God forever; it is not a temporary escape or a fleeting experience like the best of times on earth.

This world is not our ultimate home. Everything in this life is short. It's over quickly.

A roller coaster ride ends in two minutes.

Riding a great wave ends in less than 60 seconds.

Snowboarding down a mountain takes no more than three minutes.

A honeymoon or vacation is usually over in about a week.

Heaven, though, is forever. We will enjoy new and greatly improved bodies that are fit for a glorious new world. There will be no more suffering or pain. There will be no more sin and death. There will be no more guilt or shame. There will be no more depression, no more despair, and no more discouragement in heaven. The losses will end.

If you're going through a hard time, if you're discouraged, you might not feel like God's goodness and mercy are pursuing you. The promise of heaven might seem more like a distant wish-dream than a real and present help. We must learn to challenge our feelings with the truth of God's Word. Again, our natural tendency is to view life through the telephoto lens of our circumstances, and not through the wide-angle lens of God's Word.

Every day we're given is a miraculous gift. That doesn't mean that every day is easy or enjoyable. Jesus promised we would have trouble in this world. He also promised that he would be with us. That's what we see in Psalm 23—the reality of trouble and the reality of God's presence and help. This is called equal truth.

Jesus told his despairing disciples to take heart because he has overcome the world. He tells us the same thing today—to take heart. As we walk with him through this world, we will overcome everything that's thrown at us, including depression. The apostle Paul preached in Acts 13:39 that *"by him everyone who believes is freed from everything from which you could not be freed by the law of Moses."*

> **"By him everyone who believes is freed from everything from which you could not be freed by the law of Moses."**

So if you're depressed or discouraged, keep fighting the good fight of faith. Take advantage of every means of grace we've talked about in this book and trust the Lord to see you through the dark valleys. You might feel alone in your depression, but you're never truly alone. The Good Shepherd is with you. He pursues you with his goodness and mercy. And he promises a future world of love and joy and glory that more than makes up for all the pain you go through in this world.

Yes, it is Friday, but Sunday is coming.

Stay faithful!

Afterword

The motive behind the writing of this book is a simple one. Really, I wrote it for one reason and one reason only: to be an encouragement to those walking through the darkness of depression. I purposely avoided focusing too much on various treatment options and theories about depression. There's a place for that, and others have addressed those issues helpfully. My objective, rather, was to increase people's hope in a real God who loves and cares for his people.

While this book does not answer every question and cannot heal every hurt, I hope it was a fresh word of encouragement to the heart and the mind. I have prayed and continue to pray that the Lord will use this book to serve as a little patch of green pasture for the discouraged, the despairing, and the depressed.

As we come to the end of our journey together, let me quickly summarize the major themes that we covered. The message of this book revolves around three key truths found in King David's majestic song of praise to the Lord, Psalm 23:

You are not alone.
You will get through this valley.
There is purpose in the darkness.

You are not alone

Peace in the valley is found not in the absence of darkness but in the presence of our Good Shepherd. Remember, Christ came not to fix you but to save you. One of the greatest promises in the Bible is that our Shepherd is with us always. He is right there with you in the darkness. He is not just close; he actually indwells you by his Spirit. So you are never alone. When the darkness threatened to completely engulf the heart and the mind of Job, he cried out, *"Though he slay me, I will hope in him"* (Job 13:15). You too must hope in him when things seem hopeless. Faith is hoping in what we can't see—the deliverance that's coming sooner or later.

You will get through this valley

God's silence is not an indication of his absence in your life. Some of the things you long for in this life may seem to elude you, but this life is not the end of your story. The lifting of the darkness *will* happen—in this life it may only happen in part, but in eternity there will be a complete healing of every hurt and disappointment you experience. Consider that the apostle Paul lived with a thorn in the flesh that never was removed this side of heaven. Yet he found sufficient grace to live one day at a time, trusting the Lord. Today, that thorn is no longer a source of pain. Paul has not only been fixed, but he has been perfected. Keep that eternal perspective as you walk through the valley. This is not a call to live with resignation, but with biblical hope.

There is purpose in the darkness

Nothing is wasted in the valley. God redeems the time we spend in the valley. It's not random or purposeless. God sanctifies us in the valley, making us more like Christ. He considers that to be of supreme importance. Not only that, but God prepares us for service while we are in the valley. We learn dependence and humility there. We learn to empathize with others who are suffering. Spurgeon said, "The Lord gets his best soldiers out of the highlands of affliction."[1] The highlands may feel more like lowlands, but it's in these tough places that the Lord graciously sands off our rough edges and conforms us to the very image of his Son.

Just one more thing I need to say before I go. I want to encourage you with the truth that you are *not* an unusual case. Yes, no one else's circumstances and weaknesses are exactly like yours, but countless men and women before you have walked through the same kind of darkness you may be experiencing now, and many more will go through it after you're gone. Take comfort and find courage from the great cloud of witnesses surrounding you, who successfully followed the Shepherd all the way to the house of the Lord. By faith, they walked through the darkness, and you will too.

Cheering you on from a distance.

Notes

Chapter 1

1. Jack Eswine,"Listening for the Sound of Reality: The Melancholy of Abraham Lincoln and Charles Haddon Spurgeon" (Lecture, Christ Community Church, Carmel, IN, June 3, 2006).

2. Meredeth Engel, "8% of Americans Are Depressed, CDC Study Finds," *New York Daily News*, December 3, 2014, accessed October 16, 2017, http://www.nydailynews.com/life-style/health/8-americans-depressed-cdc-study-article-1.2032035.

3. Association of Certified Biblical Counselors, "Listening to Depression," September 16, 2014, accessed October 16, 2017, https://biblicalcounseling.com/2014/09/listening-to-depression/.

4. Cardwell C. Nuckols, *Diagnostic and Statistical Manual of Mental Disorders, 5th ed.* (American Psychiatric Association, 2013).

5. David P. Murray, *Christians Get Depressed Too: Hope and Help for Depressed People* (Grand Rapids, MI: Reformation Heritage Books, 2010).

6. Charles H. Spurgeon, "Jesus Wept" (sermon), in *Spurgeon's Sermons, vol. 35., Christian Classics Ethereal Library*, accessed October 12, 2017, https://www.ccel.org/ccel/spurgeon/sermons35.xxx.html.

Chapter 2

1. Dave Veerman, *365 Pocket Morning Prayers: Strength and Joy to Begin Each Day* (Barton-Veerman Company, 2016).

Chapter 3

1. "Death Valley National Park," *National Geographic Travel*, November 2, 2015, http://www.nationalgeographic.com/travel/national-parks/death-valley-national-park/.
2. Ibid.
3. Tony Evans, *Prayers for Victory in Spiritual Warfare* (Eugene, OR: Harvest House Publishers, 2015).
4. Mark Batterson, *If: Trading Your If Only Regrets for God's What If Possibilities* (Grand Rapids, MI: Baker Books), 2015.
5. Gilbert K. Chesterton, *The Innocence of Father Brown* (Pantianos Classics, 1911).
6. C. H. Spurgeon, quoted in *The Complete Works of C. H. Spurgeon, vol. 14: Sermons 788 to 847* (Delmarva Publications, 2015).
7. George Eliot, *The Daily Notes from Canonsburg, Pennsylvania*, January 24, 1906, 6.
8. G. K. Chesterton, quoted in Nancy Kennedy, *Praying with Women of the Bible* (Grand Rapids, MI: Zondervan, 2004), 116.

Chapter 4

1. Robert L. Leahy PhD, "How Big a Problem Is Anxiety?," *Psychology Today*, April 30 2008.

Chapter 5

1. John Piper, *Desiring God* (Colorado Springs, CO: Multnomah Books, 1986), 10.

Chapter 6

1. "America's Workers: Stressed Out, Overwhelmed, Totally Exhausted," *The Atlantic*, March 25, 2015, accessed October 12, 2017, https://www.theatlantic.com/business/archive/2014/03/americas-workers-stressed-out-overwhelmed-totally-exhausted/284615/.

2. Ibid.

3. W. Phillip Keller, *A Shepherd Looks at Psalm 23* (Grand Rapids, MI: Zondervan, 2007), 42.

4. Blaise Pascal, trans. A. J. Krailsheimer, *Human Happiness* (London: Penguin Books, 1995).

Chapter 7

1. Author unknown, "How Blessed Are You," accessed October 18, 2017, http://epistle.us/inspiration/blessed.html.

Chapter 9

1. Frederick William Faber, *Growth in Holiness, or, the Progress of the Spiritual Life* (London: Thomas Richardson and Son, 1854).

Chapter 10

1. *Family Circle*, November, 1999, quoted in http://www.dwlz.com/Motivation/tips42.html.

Chapter 11

1. Batterson, *If: Trading Your If Only Regrets for God's What If Possibilities* (Grand Rapids: Baker Books, 2015), 86.

2. Stephen M. Miller, *Less Stress, Please* (Kansas City: Beacon Hill Press, 1994).

3. General Jim Mattis, quoted in Frank Miniter, "The Surprising Thing About Gen. 'Mad Dog' Mattis That Could Add a Manly Dose To American Culture," December 5, 2016, https://www.forbes.com/sites/frankminiter/2016/12/05/the-surprising-thing-about-gen-mad-dog-mattis-that-could-add-a-manly-dose-to-american-culture/#65588ae17b64.

Chapter 12

1. *Praise Reports: Inspiring Real-Life Stories of How God Answers Prayer*, Crosswalk.com, 2009.

Chapter 13

1. A.W. Tozer, *The Knowledge of the Holy* (New York: HarperCollins, 1961), 1.

Chapter 14

1. C.S. Lewis, quoted in Lauren Mitchell, *Steadfast: A Study of the Prayer That Made David's Whole Heart Rely on a Steadfast God* (Nashville, TN: CrossBooks, 2014), 99.

2. "Top 18 Chip Ingram Quotes," *Hear It First*, accessed 12 Oct 2017, http://www.hearitfirst.com/news/top-18-chip-ingram-quotes.

Afterword

1. Martin H. Manser, ed. *The Westminster Collection of Christian Quotations* (Louisville: Westminster John Knox Press, 2001), 382.

CPSIA information can be obtained
at www.ICGtesting.com
Printed in the USA
FSHW010651111219
64730FS